Ammeter

Voltmeter

Eyewitness
Electricity

Written by
STEVE PARKER

Tube of pure potassium produced by
electrolysis by Humphry Davy (1807)

Early telegraph cables encased in wood (1837)

Making a wire
glow red hot using
a battery (1895)

D0995710

Telephone handset (1895)

DK

LONDON, NEW YORK, MELBOURNE, MUNICH, AND DELHI

Project Editor Charyn Jones
Senior Art Editor Neville Graham
Design Assistant Marianna Papachrysanthou
DTP Manager Joanna Figg-Latham
Production Eunice Paterson
Managing Editor Josephine Buchanan
Special Photography Clive Streeter
Editorial Consultant Neil Brown, Science Museum, London

REVISED EDITION
Revised by Steve Parker

DK INDIA
Project editor Shatarupa Chaudhuri
Project art editor Nishesh Batnagar
Assistant editor Priyanka Kharbanda
Art editor Honlung Zach Ragui
DTP designer Tarun Sharma
Picture researcher Sumedha Chopra

DK UK
Senior editor Caroline Stamps
Senior art editor Rachael Grady
Pre-production producers Adam Stoneham, Rachel Ng
Publisher Andrew Macintyre

This Eyewitness ® Guide has been conceived by
Dorling Kindersley Limited and Editions Gallimard
First published in Great Britain in 1992
This revised edition published in 2013
by Dorling Kindersley Limited, 80 Strand, London WC2R 0RL

10 9 8 7 6 5 4 3 2 1
001 – 187809 – July/13

A CIP catalogue record for this book is
available from the British Library.

ISBN: 978-1-40932-558-1

Colour reproduction by Colourscan, Singapore
Printed and bound in China by South China Printing Co. Ltd

Discover more at
www.dk.com

Damaged
lightning
conductor
(1916)

10,000 volt electrici
cable insulated wit
waxed paper (1890

Interior
of carbon
arc lamp
(1870–80)

G·ADAMS
LONDON

Pith ball
electrometer
(19th century)

Contents

Brass-cased switch (1920)

A mysterious force

SINCE THE BEGINNING OF THE UNIVERSE, there was electricity. Even when there was no life on our planet, more than 4,000 million years ago, great bolts of lightning lit up the skies. Lightning is one of nature's most dramatic demonstrations of the energy form we call electricity. As life evolved, electricity became a vital part of the living world. It forms the basis of a nerve signal. Eyes receive light rays and turn them into tiny electrical signals that pass along nerves into the brain and from there to the rest of the body. Our whole awareness and ability to think and move depends on tiny electrical signals whizzing around the nerve pathways inside the brain. In the past few centuries, scientists have gradually begun to unravel the mysteries of electricity. Their advances were often linked to progress in other areas of science. Following this scientific research, came exploitation. Inventors used electrical energy to serve our needs (pp. 46–49).

Thales of Miletus

ATTRACTION
Some of the earliest known scientific experiments were carried out by people such as Thales (below left) in ancient Greece. If a piece of amber (the gum or resin from trees, which has fossilized and turned solid) is rubbed briskly with a piece of wool or fur, and brought near to a light object such as a feather, the feather flies up and clings to the amber. The word "electricity" comes from *elektron*, the Greek term for amber.

Amber

Feather flies up as though lifted by an invisible hand

Feathers are light enough to be attracted to the amber

Charge is gradually lost, the amber loses its attraction and the feathers float down

THE VIEWS OF THE ANCIENTS
The Ancient Greeks were among the first thinkers in the scientific tradition. One of the earliest Greek scientists was Thales of Miletus (c. 625–547 BCE) who was a skillful mathematician. None of Thales' own writings survive, but reports of his work show that he is believed to have carried out simple experiments into the effects of what we now call electricity and magnetism.

ELECTRICITY IN THE AIR

The lightning bolt is an awesome example of electricity in action. The explanations of what electricity is, where it comes from, and how it works are central to our understanding of matter and the fundamental forces of nature. Lightning is the result of the discharge of an electric charge in a cloud. The energy of the discharge is so great that it produces an intense trail of light, heat, and sound – thunder. It can destroy buildings, kill humans, and consume trees in a sheet of flame. Observations of lightning led scientists and thinkers such as Benjamin Franklin (pp. 8–9) to investigate and begin to unravel the mysteries of electric charge.

PLAYING TRICKS

In times gone by, teachers showed the attraction of magnetic and electrically charged objects, even though they did not understand their nature. Magicians still use the attracting powers of magnetism and "static" electricity (or electric charge) in their acts.

ELECTRICITY IN THE HUMAN BODY

Human life depends on electricity. About every second, tiny electrical signals spread through the heart muscle, triggering and coordinating a heartbeat. These signals send "echoes" through the body tissues to the skin. Here they can be detected by metal sensors and displayed as a wavy line called the electrocardiogram (p. 51).

ELECTRICITY IN ANIMALS

In the animal world, a busy muscle produces small pulses of electricity. Creatures have capitalized on this for hunting and killing. The electric ray has modified muscle blocks on either side of its head. These jelly-like "living batteries" send shock waves through the water to stun or kill a nearby victim. A typical shark has 1,000 electricity-sensing pits in its skin, mainly around its head. They pick up tiny electrical pulses from the active muscles of fish. A shark can home in on its meal with complete accuracy even in complete darkness by using its electrical-navigation sensors.

Electricity-producing muscle blocks

Nerves controlling electric organs

Atlantic torpedo or electric ray

Shark

Ideas about electricity

IN THE EARLY DAYS of experiments with electricity, scientists had no batteries to make electricity. Instead, they made it themselves by rubbing certain materials together. In about 1600 William Gilbert suggested there were two kinds of electricity, based on the material used for rubbing, though he did not know why this was so. Glass rubbed with silk made vitreous electricity, and amber rubbed with fur made resinous electricity. His experiments showed that objects containing the same kind of electricity repelled each other, while those containing different kinds attracted each other (pp. 10–11). Benjamin Franklin also believed that there were two kinds of electricity. He proposed that electrical charge was like "fluid" spreading itself through an object. It could jump to another object, making a spark.

Versorium

Finely balanced thin pointer of light wood

Upright rod

GILBERT'S VERSORIUM
William Gilbert (1544–1603) was a doctor to Queen Elizabeth I of England. In 1600 he wrote about the mysterious forces of magnetism and electricity in his book *De Magnete* (*On the Magnet*). Gilbert was the first person to use the word "electric", and he invented possibly the earliest electrical instrument, the versorium. Objects like paper and straw, which had an electrical charge when rubbed, made the pointer of the versorium swing towards them. He called these attracting substances "electrics". Those that did not attract the pointer were "nonelectrics".

Tip bent by intense heat

Lightning conductor

Charge-collecting metal combs

Charge conducted down chains to jars

Leyden jar

Outer metal casing of Leyden jar

Brus touc acro disc part cha buil

DIRECT HIT
A lightning bolt is a giant spark of electric charge jumping from a thunder-cloud to the ground. If lightning hits anything, it burns it. A conductor directs lightning through a copper strip to the earth, leaving the building safe.

A RISKY EXPERIMENT
The lightning experiments of Benjamin Franklin (1706–90) were copied by other investigators. The scientist Georg Richmann at St Petersburg, Russia, was killed by the electric charge of lightning when he held a wire-tipped pole up high in a storm. The sparks from lightning were in fact similar to those obtained in laboratories.

BENJAMIN FRANKLIN
To "collect" electricity from lightning, Franklin is said to have flown a kite in a thunderstorm. Electricity flowed down the wet line and produced a small spark, showing that lightning bolts were huge electric sparks.

PRODUCING ELECTRIC CHARGE

For many years, the Wimshurst machine was used to produce electric charge. The machine works by induction (p. 11). Turning the crank handle starts a process involving the metal sectors which are stuck on the outside of two glass discs – one wheel rotates in the opposite direction to the other – and metal combs that point to the discs, but do not actually touch them. This process multiplies small stray electric charge many times. The charge produced is stored in Leyden jars. When enough charge has built up, it jumps between the two discharging spheres, producing a bright spark. The device was developed by James Wimshurst (1832–1903). Wimshurst machines were used to demonstrate making static electricity – as the charge is sometimes called – until at least the 1960s. The largest machine had discs that were 2.12 m (7 ft) in diameter.

James Wimshurst

Discharging spheres

Wimshurst machine (1882)

As the charge builds up, a spark leaps across the small gap

Conductor arms

Metal sectors stuck to outside of both discs

Two contra-rotating glass discs placed close together

Metal combs point to sectors on glass discs and collect charge

Pulley

Crossed drive belt

Drive belt

Leyden jar

Hand-turned crank handle

Drive pulley

Metal ball

Leyden jar being discharged

Discharger rod

Spark

Lid

Glass jar

Outer metal coating

Metal ball

Lid

STORING CHARGE

The Leyden jar was an early device scientists used for storing the electric charge they were making. It is named after the place where it was developed in 1746 – the University of Leyden in the Netherlands. The electric charge flows down the metal chain to the metal coating inside the jar. It cannot leak away through the glass jar, so it builds up. If the discharger rod is held near the jar (above), the charge leaps from the ball on top, through the discharger to the outer metal coating on the jar – causing a spark. The Leyden jar was an early type of capacitor (pp. 12–13).

Metal chain

Glass jar

Outer metal coating

Leyden jar with lid and chain

The quest for knowledge

DURING THE 18TH CENTURY many scientists experimented with electric charge in their laboratories. As yet, there were no practical uses for electricity; what interested scientists was the quest for knowledge. They observed how electric charge could be seen as sparks, and how it behaved differently with different substances. Since electricity was invisible, instruments were needed to detect and measure it. Initially, progress was haphazard. There was no way to make a sustained flow of electric charge – that came later from the battery (pp. 16–19). Startling new discoveries were made that are now taken for granted. For instance, in the 1720s the English scientist Stephen Gray (1666–1736) proposed that any object which touches an "electrified (charged) body will itself become electrified". Charge transferring from one substance to another one that touches it is a process known as electrical conduction.

JOSEPH PRIESTLEY
Before achieving fame as a chemist and the discoverer of oxygen, Priestley (1733–1804) was interested in electricity. In 1767 he published the earliest history of electrical science – *The History and Present State of Electricity*. This was his personal assessment of contemporary studies.

Electrostatic machine

Friction from leather pressing on glass produces electric charge

Electric charge can jump from the metal ball as a spark

Electric charge collected by comb-shaped metal collector

Electric charge can stored in th Leyden jar

Hand-turned crank causes glass cylinder to revolve

GENERATING ELECTRIC CHARGE
Electrostatic generators, first developed by English experimenter Francis Hauksbee (c. 1660–1713) in 1710, generated larger and larger amounts of electric charge. They were used by scientists experimenting with the nature of electricity, and also in public to produce bigger sparks for amazed audiences. This machine was one of those made by the successful scientific instrument maker George Adams (1750–95).

Horse and rider electrostatic toy

Charge sprays off the end of the point

Vanes spin

Connection to source of charge

Rider and horse go round

MOVING TOYS
Electric charge was used to work this country scene from the mid-19th century. The metal point was connected to a source of charge; the charge "sprayed" off the end of the point and jumped to the vanes, moving them and the model around.

DEMONSTRATION HOUSE
Wooden houses such as the one in th engraving were used to demonstrate how a lightning conductor works. The walls and roof were made to fall apart easily. Hidden inside was a container of gunpowder. Electric charge from an electrostatic generator representing lightning, would norma be guided down into the earth by a metal lightning conductor. If this was disconnected in the model, the charg created a spark that set off the gunpowder, blowing off the roof so the walls fell flat.

Positively charged resin rod

Charged electroscope

Uncharged electroscope

Gold leaves close when uncharged

Metal plate attracts negative charge

Protective insulation around metal rod

Earthed metal frame inside container

Charles de Coulomb

Records from Coulomb's memoirs (1784)

LAW OF ELECTRICAL FORCE

In the 1780s French physicist Charles de Coulomb (1736–1806) was one of the first scientists to measure how electric charge behaved. He did this by observing the attracting or repelling forces they exerted, by measuring the twist in a thread or wire. He adapted the torsion balance, which was used to weigh light objects. The object's weight acted as a turning force to twist a thread. The amount of twist was in proportion to the object's weight. In Coulomb's delicate instrument, the torsional force came from electric charge on one fixed sphere repelling a movable sphere. After many experiments, Coulomb proposed the inverse square law: the force of attraction or repulsion between two charged objects changes according to the ratio of the squares of their distance apart.

Torsion balance

Knob for adjusting the resting position of the swinging ball

Upper fixed ball can be charged

Metal bar suspended by fine silk thread

Lower ball shares charge with the upper ball

Movable ball balanced by weight at other end

Scale for measuring the position of the swinging ball

Protective container keeps out currents of air

·TECTING CHARGE
· gold leaf
·troscope was an
·ortant instrument
· detecting electric
·rge. Usually it
·ked by electrical
·uction. To induce
·arge, a positively
·rged resin rod is
· near to the top
·he electroscope. It
·acts the negative
·rge up the metal
· in the jar. This
·es an excess of
·itive charge on the
· leaves attached to
·bottom of the rod.
·e the gold leaves
·e the same charge,
·y repel each other,
· so move apart. At
·time scientists did
·fully understand
· the electroscope
·ked because they
· not yet discovered
· there were two
·es of charge –
·itive and negative
·20–21).

·rged gold
·es repel
· other

·ss case protects
·ves from air
·vements

11

Collecting electric charge

Today, CHARGE-PRODUCING ELECTROSTATIC GENERATORS are an unfamiliar sight, confined to museums and research laboratories. These machines were designed to produce large charges and extremely high voltages. Charge-storing devices are vital components found inside many electrical devices, from washing machines to mobile phones. They used to be known as condensers but are now called capacitors. There are many different types of capacitor (opposite), yet they all use the same principle as the Leyden jar (pp. 8–9), the first electrical storage container. Capacitors are among the few electric devices, such as batteries, that can store electrical charge. They are also used to separate alternating current (a.c.) from direct current (d.c.).

THE SPARK OF LIFE
The electrostatic generator's giant sparks made impressive special effects at the movies. Their similarity to lightning bolts fitted neatly into the plot of Mary Shelley's horror story *Frankenstein*. Doctor Frankenstein's monster, made from sewn-together parts of dead bodies, is jolted into life by the shock from a lightning bolt.

VAN DE GRAAFF GENERATOR
American scientist Robert Van de Graaff (1901–67) developed a machine in the early 1930s for collecting and storing huge amounts of electric charge. He is shown here with one of his smaller electrostatic generators. The charge in the machine, which is named after him, builds up on a metal sphere, and reaches an incredible 10 million volts. The machine is mostly used as a research tool for studying the particles that make up atoms. The vast energy represented by its accumulated charge is transferred to the atoms' particles by accelerating the particles to enormous speed, so that scientists can study their interactions as they smash together.

Robert Van de Graaff

SPEEDING PARTICLES
The Cockcroft–Walton generator at Brookhaven Laboratory on Long Island, New York, USA, generates electrical energy in the form of ultra-high voltages. The energy speeds up parts of atoms so fast that they travel a distance equivalent to the Moon and back in four seconds.

ACCUMULATING CHARGE
In the Van de Graaff generator (below), the source of positive electric charge is a comb-shaped charge-sprayer connected to the electricity supply. The charge is carried on a moving belt to a charge collector above. This transfers it to the exterior of the large metal sphere. The sphere is mounted on a column that prevents the charge from leaking away. In atomic research there are no sparks; the fast-moving sub-atomic particles carry the charge away. In public demonstrations, such as this model at the Boston Museum of Science in the United States (right), the accumulated charge leaps across to another piece of metal nearby, with a giant spark like a mini-lightning bolt.

How the Van de Graaff works

- Sphere
- Charge collector
- Tube in which sub-atomic particles can be accelerated
- Moving belt
- Charge-spraying comb
- Electricity supply

Capacitors

There are many different types of capacitor that store electric charge. Two sheets of metal, or a similar electrical conductor, are separated by an insulating material such as paper or air. In a Leyden jar, the glass of the jar is the separating substance. Capacitance is measured in units called farads after Michael Faraday (pp. 34–35). One farad is a huge amount of charge, and most modern capacitors are fingertip-sized items rated at microfarads (millionths of a farad) or less.

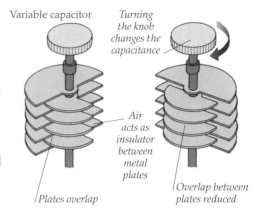

Variable capacitor

Turning the knob changes the capacitance

Air acts as insulator between metal plates

Plates overlap

Overlap between plates reduced

CAPACITORS AT WORK

In electrical devices, a capacitor is used to store charge and release it at a certain moment, or to resist the continuous flow of charge through it. Bigger conducting plates, and a narrower gap between them, increases the amount of charge stored. The tuning knob on this 1950s radio operates a variable capacitor, altering the overlap between its stack of metal plates. This changes the capacitance and causes the radio to respond to signals of a different frequency, that is, to pick up a different radio station.

Metal plates of variable capacitor

Tuning knob

Using charges

THE DUST RESTING on a television screen is an example of electrostatic attraction. The surface of the screen becomes electrically charged while the television is on. It then attracts and holds any floating specks that happen to come near. This phenomenon of electrostatic forces, where there is attraction by unlike charges, and repulsion by like ones, is put to work in a variety of modern machines and processes. For instance, in the body-painting shop of a car manufacturer, tiny droplets of spray paint are all given the same electric charge. They repel each other and are attracted towards the car's body, and so settle on it as a more even coating. This is exactly the same principle as the charge that amber, when rubbed, produces to pick up feathers (pp. 6–7).

THE CARLSON COPIER
In 1938 American lawyer Chester Carlson (1906–68) devised a process known as electrophotography. He wanted a machine that could duplicate patent application forms – not only the words, but also complicated drawings. He invented an electrostatic printer, or xerography machine, (from the Greek words *xeros* meaning "dry", and *graphos* for "writing"). The first xerographic print (above) was made by Carlson in 1938, but the first commercial copies were not produced until the 1950s.

Carlson's first print

Carlson with his early copier

Xerox copier (1960)

Charging chamber with top removed

Out[er] casi[ng]

Selenium coated pl[ate]

Charging w[ire]

Plate-charging button

Edge of selenium-coated plate

Developing tray with toner inside

Special toner tray (used for copying half-tone pictures)

"DRY WRITING"
The Xerox copier uses the attraction of unlike electric charges (pp. 10–11). At its heart is a special metal plate coated with a substance called selenium. A pattern of positive charges on the plate, representing the black areas to be copied, attracts negatively charged particles of a fine black powder – the toner. (The toner becomes negatively charged by contact with tiny glass beads in the developing tray.) The toner pattern is transferred to a blank sheet of paper and heat-sealed in place. In a modern copier, the selenium-coated plate is on a rotating drum. Otherwise the process is much the same as this 1960s machine, but now it happens automatically.

TONE TRAY

king a
otocopy

Light must be kept out until the developing stage is complete

Plate is locked in developing tray

Plate in charging chamber is positively charged

Selenium-coated plate with toner adhering to it

CHARGING AND EXPOSING THE PLATE
The selenium-coated plate is put in the charging chamber and, as the electrified wires go over, it receives an even coating of positive charges. The protective shield is replaced and the plate removed to a camera, where it is exposed to the document to be copied. An image of the document is shone on to it by a camera lens. Where light hits the plate, from the white areas of the original document, the selenium becomes a conductor, and the charge flows away. Where no light reaches, the charge remains.

2 DEVELOPING THE PLATE
The plate now has an exact mirror copy of the original document on its surface, in the form of a pattern of positive electrostatic charge. With the protective shield in place the plate is locked to the developing tray. The shield is removed, and the plate swings backwards and forwards. As this happens the toner in the developing tray cascades over the plate. Its tiny negatively charged grains are attracted to the positively charged areas of the plate, where they stick.

3 THE DEVELOPED IMAGE
The plate is removed from the developer tray. This reveals the selenium-coated plate with the fine powder adhering to it, as an exact but mirror-image replica of the original document. The plate is returned to the charging chamber.

plate and paper slid into the charging chamber

The paper now holds a duplicate of the original

The paper is baked in the fuser

4 POWDER TO PAPER
The next stage also depends on electrostatic attraction. A sheet of blank paper is placed over the plate and its powder image. The plate and paper are pushed back into the charging chamber and withdrawn again while the transfer switch is depressed. The paper becomes positively charged so that it attracts the toner powder away from the plate.

5 REMOVING THE COPY
The paper is carefully lifted from the plate, bringing with it the pattern of toner, which is now stuck to it by electrostatic attraction. The copied parts have been reversed again, so that they are an exact duplicate of the original.

6 HEAT-SEALING THE COPY
Finally, the plain paper with its powder pattern is placed on the fuser tray and pushed into an oven-like chamber for a few seconds. The powder bakes and melts into the fibres of the paper, permanently sealing the image. The entire process takes about three minutes – much longer than the couple of seconds in a modern photocopier.

DUST-EATING AIR FILTER
The electrostatic air filter on this 1930s cigarette card, showing a man demonstrating the filter with cigarette smoke, uses a fan to draw in a stream of dusty, impure air. A prefilter traps the bigger floating particles. The remaining small ones pass through the first electrified grid of a device called the electrostatic precipitator. This grid gives each particle a negative charge. The particles are repelled from the negative wires on to the precipitator's second, positively charged grid. They are attracted to it, and stick to its mesh. A filter then absorbs any odours and cleaned air blows out the other end.

How an electrostatic precipitator works

Prefilter traps large particles

Negatively charged grid

Positively charged mesh

Charcoal filter absorbs leftover odours

A flow of charge

In 1780, while Italian anatomist Luigi Galvani (1737–98) was dissecting and studying a frog, he noticed that when his sharp scalpel touched the nerves in the frog's leg, the leg twitched. Galvani suspected that there was electricity in the frog's muscles, and experimented to explain what he had seen. Soon another Italian, Alessandro Volta (1745–1827), heard of the incident. Volta disagreed with Galvani's ideas. He had already developed a device for producing small amounts of electric charge – the electrophorus. In 1800 he announced that he had found a new source of electricity, one which produced electricity continuously (unlike the Leyden jar which discharged instantly). It became known as the voltaic pile. Galvani thought electricity came from animals' bodies when touched by two metals, calling it "animal electricity". Volta thought it came from contact between metals only; he called it "metallic electricity". Galvani and Volta disagreed strongly, and they and their supporters argued for years. We now know that neither was totally correct.

Galvani's laboratory

Voltaic pile

Glass supporting rod

THE VOLTAIC PILE
This device used two different metals, separated by moist chemicals, to produce a flow of electric charge. The original voltaic pile used three types of disc: zinc, pasteboard or leather, and copper. The pasteboard was soaked in a solution of salt or weak acid such as vinegar. In an electrochemical reaction, the copper loses electrons (p. 20) to the solution and the zinc gains electrons from the solution. At the same time, zinc dissolves and hydrogen gas is produced at the surface of the copper. When the charge flows away along wires, the chemicals separate out more charge. And so electric charge continues to flow. Volta had invented the earliest electric cell. He piled up many of these cells or three-disc units to strengthen the effect. In this way he produced the first battery, which is a collection of cells (pp. 18–19).

Copper disc

Zinc disc

Pasteboard disc

Wooden base

LUIGI GALVANI
Galvani studied the effects of electric charge from Leyden jars and electrostatic machines on animals. In a number of ways Galvani brought animal tissue into contact with two metals in his laboratory (above). He noticed convulsions in the limbs of the dead animals. Chemicals in the nerves and muscles, when placed between the metals, had caused an electrochemical reaction (pp. 18–19), making an electric cell.

Luigi Galvani

essandro
lta

SSANDRO VOLTA

20 March 1800 Volta sketched a U-shaped
aic pile in a letter to Sir Joseph Banks,
ident of the Royal Society of London.
pile was the first practical
ery. The modern unit of
trical potential, which
e strength or "electrical
" of the flowing charge,
e volt (p. 25), named
onour of Volta. His
aratus produced just
one volt for every
of discs. The electric
p. 7) can send a
-volt shock through
water. A modern
se mains circuit
es 110 or 220 volts
high-voltage power
carry up to half a
on volts or more.

STORING CHARGE
The insulating base of the electrophorus, which was
made from a resinous substance, was negatively charged
by rubbing it so that when the metal plate was placed on
top of it, the bottom of the disc acquired a positive charge,
while the top was negatively charged. The negative
charge was drained away by touching the plate (above)
and the positively charged plate could then be taken
away, and the charge on it used.

THE ELECTROPHORUS
Volta invented the
electrophorus in 1775.
It consisted of a metal plate,
which could be charged,
placed on an insulating
base. With a handle, which
was also made from an
insulating material, the
electrophorous could be
used as a portable carrier
of electric charge, to transfer
charge to another apparatus,
or further charge a Leyden
jar. The process of charging
and discharging the
electrophorus could be
repeated indefinitely.

Glass handle

Brass disc carries the charge

*Ebonite base which
can be charged*

Sets of discs

Insulated wire

Wire inserted under disc

Components of a voltaic cell

Zinc disc

Salt-soaked pasteboard disc

Copper disc

Copper disc

Zinc disc

WIRING UP THE BATTERY
To connect up the voltaic pile to a
piece of equipment, two insulated
copper wires were attached to sets
of discs. With 24 sets of discs this
battery produced about 24 volts,
which Volta detected with the tip of
his tongue on the connecting wires.

Electricity from chemicals

RESEARCHERS FOUND THAT THE SIMPLEST electricity-making unit, or electric cell, was two plates of different metals in a jar filled with liquid. The metal plates are called electrodes. They are conductors through which electricity can enter or leave. The positive electrode is called the anode and the negative electrode is called the cathode. The liquid, which must be able to conduct electricity, is called the electrolyte. Several cells joined together form a battery. There have been many types and sizes of cells and batteries. Some of them used strong acids or other noxious chemicals as the electrolyte. The first batteries supplied electricity for research, in the laboratory. Large numbers of batteries were used for electric telegraphs (pp. 56–57). An important advance was the "dry" cell, a development of the Leclanché cell (below), which uses a jelly-like paste instead of liquid. More recent advances include alkaline and other long-life cells.

SECONDARY CELLS
Secondary or rechargeable batteries were developed in 1859 by French scientist Gaston Planté (1834–89). In a primary cell, such as a torch battery, the chemical reactions eventually become spent and no longer produce electricity. In a secondary cell, the reactions can be reversed by electricity from another source. After recharging, the cell produces current again.

Terminal

Leclanché cell

Carbon rod

Zinc rod

Glass jar

Electrolyte in jar – ammonium chloride solution

Zinc cathode

Corrosion-resistant glass container

Central part of Leclanché cell

Terminal

Carbon rod

Manganese dioxide and carbon granules

THE CELL AT WORK
A basic electrical cell has copper and zinc plates immersed in sulphuric acid. When the plates are connected by a conducting wire, chemical reactions occur. Hydrogen gas is given off at the copper plate, which loses electrons (p. 33) to the solution, becoming positively charged. Zinc dissolves from the zinc plate, leaving behind electrons that make the plate negative. The electrons move through the wire from the zinc plate towards the copper. This constitutes the electric current, which continues until the zinc is eaten away or the acid used up.

LECLANCHE CELL
During the 1860s French chemist Georges Leclanché (1839–82) devised a cell in which one electrode was a zinc rod, and the other was a carbon rod inside a pot of manganese dioxide and carbon granules. Between was a solution of ammonium chloride. The cell produced about 1.5 volts. It did not contain dangerous acid, and it soon became a popular and relatively portable electricity-maker, and the forerunner of the torch battery.

MASSIVE BATTERY
Humphry Davy
(1778–1829) was
professor at London's
Royal Institution.
In 1807 he used a
roomful of batteries,
some 2,000 cells in
all, to make enough
electricity to produce
pure potassium metal
by the process of
electrolysis (pp. 32–33).

HIGH-TENSION BATTERY

This 1920s lead-acid storage battery was used to provide electricity for a domestic radio set. "High tension" means that the electricity had a high pressure, that is, a large voltage. Each glass jar contained two lead plates and the electrolyte – dilute sulphuric acid. The battery was recharged at the local garage, where batteries used in the new and popular automobiles were maintained, by being connected to an electricity supply to reverse the chemical reaction. It was then topped up with water to compensate for any water loss through evaporation.

High-tension battery without lid

Copper anode

Wire carries electric current

Wooden case

Glass containers – each one a single cell

Sulphuric acid

Connecting bars

Swinging bar lifts electrodes up when battery not in use

Hydrogen gas

PORTABLE LIGHT TO READ BY

A safe, portable battery, combined with the electric light bulb (pp. 46–47), supplied light wherever it was needed. This late 19th-century train traveller reads with the battery in the bag by his side.

Sealed top-up hole

1940s car battery

Terminal

THE CAR BATTERY

These rechargeable, lead-acid batteries are known as accumulators. Each cell consists of two lead plates, or electrodes, separated by sulphuric acid. As the battery is charged, lead oxide forms on one of the plates, storing the incoming electrical energy in chemical form.

DANIELL CELL

English professor John Daniell (1790–1845) developed a simple cell in 1836 that provided current for a longer period. His cell (right) had a copper cylinder as the positive electrode (anode) in copper sulphate, and a zinc rod as the negative electrode (cathode) in sulphuric acid, separated by a porous pot. It produced about one volt and supplied electricity for research.

Sulphuric acid fills void

Cell divider

Lead oxide plate

Lead metal plate

Circuits and conductors

As SCIENTISTS EXPERIMENTED with batteries, they discovered that some substances let electric charge pass through them without difficulty, while others would not. The former were called conductors, and the latter insulators. But why do some substances conduct? It is because all matter is made of atoms. An atom, in turn, is made of particles called electrons (pp. 54–55), orbiting around a central nucleus. Each electron has a negative charge, and the nucleus has balancing positive charges. An electric current occurs when the electrons move. Certain substances, especially metals, have electrons that are not tightly held to their nuclei. These "free electrons" are more mobile, and they can be set in one-way motion easily, to produce an electric current.

HENRY CAVENDISH
Forgetful and reclusive, Cavendish (1731–1810) was a great experimenter. His electrical research was wide ranging, and like other scientists of the time, he assessed the intensity of electricity by how severely he was shocked by it. One of Cavendish's theories was the idea of electrical potential or voltage to explain how the "push" of the electricity was produced.

INSIDE A CONDUCTOR
Metals are good conductors. In a good conductor, each atom has one or more free electrons. The nucleus cannot hold on to them strongly, and they can move within the conductors. Normally this happens at random, and there is no overall one-way flow of electrons. But if there is a difference in voltage between one end of the conductor and the other, the negative electrons are attracted to the positive end and so the current flows.

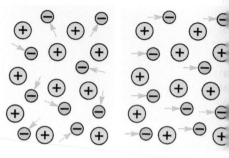

Electrons move at random

Flow of electrons producing current

MAKING A CIRCUIT
A cell or battery on its own does not produce an electric current. Electrons flow only if they have somewhere to go, and if a voltage pushes them. When conductors link one terminal of a battery to the other, a current flows. This series of conductors is a circuit. In an open or broken circuit, there is a break along the line, and the current stops. In a closed or complete circuit (right), the electrons flow from the negative side of the battery to the positive side. They can then do work, such as producing light.

Open circuit

Break in the line

Closed circuit

Battery

Platinum plate in nitric acid

Zinc plate in sulphuric acid

Wire conductor covered with textile insulation

Current makes high-resistance wire glow

Carrying current

Early experiments on conductors and insulators showed that most metals were good at carrying current. Soon, wires of iron or, even better, copper and silver were being used in electrical research. Some forms of carbon, such as graphite (the "lead" in a pencil) and charcoal were also conductors (p. 37). So was any watery substance, from solutions of acids and salts, to parts of vegetables and animals. Insulators tended to be woody, fibrous, or made of minerals. An early list of insulators included leather, parchment, ashes, chalk, hair, porcelain, feathers, precious stones, dried vegetables, resin, and amber.

A good conductor

A poor conductor

Charcoal conducts the charge away rapidly

Wool conducts the charge away very slowly

TESTING CONDUCTORS
An electroscope can show whether a substance is a conductor or an insulator. Charged from a Leyden jar or electrostatic generator, its two gold leaves repel each other and move apart. Then the test substance is held in the hand, against the metal cap. If the substance is a good conductor, it conducts the charge away from the electroscope, to the body and then into the earth. The leaves lose their charge and flop back down. The speed with which they come to rest together show how fast their charge is conducted away, and so indicates the efficiency of the conductor.

Gold leaves lose their charge and close together

Porous pot

Gold leaves keep their charge and repel each other

INSULATING PLUGS
For safety's sake, the outside of a plug must be well insulated from the conducting metal prongs inside. Bodies of early plugs were made of wood and porcelain. Bakelite, a synthetic resin and a good insulator, came into use in the 1910s.

Bakelite body (1930)

Wooden body (1915)

Porcelain body (1920)

WEATHERPROOF INSULATION
High-voltage power lines must be well insulated or the electricity may force its way through a poor insulator or spark across a gap. Porous materials, such as wood, are not used because they can absorb moisture. Non-porous substances, such as ceramics and glass, are shaped to keep rain, dew, and other moisture from creating a circuit into the earth.

Ceramic insulator (1956)

Toughened glass suspension insulator (1956)

20th-century porcelain insulator for telegraph wires

Aluminium power line

Resisting electricity

In a series of experiments around 1825 the German scientist Georg Ohm (1789–1854) demonstrated that there were no perfect electrical conductors. Each type of substance, even the best metals, put up some resistance to the current. Ohm showed that a long wire had more resistance than a short one of the same metal, and thin wires had more resistance than fat ones. Also, in a circuit, the greater the resistance, the more potential difference (volts) was needed to push the current through the wire. The relationships between potential difference, current, and resistance became known as Ohm's law.

ADJUSTABLE RESISTANCE
Scientists needing to vary the current in a circuit developed adjustable resistors, or rheostats. (These were once used in dimmer switches.) One simple design used special resistance wire, made from a combination of metals, such as nickel and copper. This put up some resistance to the current, but not too much. A long piece of the resistance wire was wound as a coil on an insulating tube. This was more convenient than having it stretched out straight. The wire touched a contact that slid along the top. Electricity from a battery came in through one terminal, then into the resistance coil. As the contact slid one way, the electricity went through more resistance wire, so the rheostat's resistance rose. As the contact moved the other way, its resistance fell.

Ammeter shows larger current

Sliding contact is a short distance along the tube

Rheostat

Wire to battery

Wire connecting rheostat to battery

Insulating tube

Ammeter

1 LOWER RESISTANCE
Electricity passes through only a short length of resistance wire, then through the top bar to the red wire. The circuit has a low overall resistance, so a large current flows, as shown on the meter.

Ammeter shows smaller current

Sliding contact half way along the tube

2 HIGHER RESISTANCE
The electricity now flows through more resistance wire. (The bar and other wires have hardly any resistance.) The circuit has a higher overall resistance, so a smaller current flows, as shown on the meter.

Georg Ohm

Ohm's practical experiments showed the mathematical links between resistance, potential difference, and current. Ohm's law of 1826 states that provided the temperature does not change, the current flowing through certain conductors is proportional to the potential difference (voltage) across it. This is written as I (current) = V (voltage) divided by R (resistance) and is now a cornerstone of electrical circuit design.

Torsion head twists to bring magnetic needle back to zero

Suspension wire

OHM'S APPARATUS
To test his theory, Ohm used a thermocouple (below), which produced a small voltage when there was a temperature difference between the junctions of two metals (pp. 52–53). To measure the current through the wire under test, he used a torsion balance similar to the one used by Coulomb (p. 11). In this reconstruction of his apparatus, he measured the deflection of the magnetized needle.

Magnetized needle turned by current in copper bar

Cold junction of thermocouple

Hot junction of thermocouple

Magnifying glass to detect swing of the needle

Copper bar

Bismuth bar

Cups of mercury into which ends of resistor are dipped

Container for ice

Boiler producing steam

led istance re

Metal bar

THE SEARCH FOR BETTER CONDUCTORS
With a knowledge of resistance, engineers could improve the design of long-distance electrical and communication cables. Better conductors surrounded by better insulators would carry higher currents farther, without expensive loss of electricity. Copper was the preferred conductor. After silver, it has the lowest resistance; it does not rust or corrode like iron or steel; and it is easily drawn out into a wire.

Power cable (20th century)

Copper cores

Flexible lead sheath

Paper insulation

STANDARD RESISTOR
After Ohm's work revealed the importance of resistance, standard resistors like this were made. It was connected up in an electrical circuit and measurements were made to calculate the resistance using Ohm's law. In 1861 the British Association Standards Committee was set up to determine the most convenient unit for resistance. It was adopted in 1865. Later, it was named "ohm" with the symbol Ω.

Brass casing for resistance wire

Copper connecting leads

Wooden storage box

Telegraph cable (1837)

Resin

Wood

Copper cores

Measuring and quantifying

In the middle of the 19th century scientists were busy studying electricity and its effects. They experimented with new types of cells and batteries, and with circuits containing different components. There was still no widespread commercial use for electricity, except for the telegraph (pp. 56–57). As with all scientific research, the experimenters had to find ways of measuring, recording, and checking their work. New measuring devices were needed and meters of ingenious design were used by the researchers who struggled to understand this mysterious "force". To make measuring devices useful, new units were devised and named. The existing units, such as metres and grams, were no use for the flowing charge of an electric current.

Wires connected to measured supply of electricity

JOULE'S LAW
An electric current flowing through a high-resistance wire heats the wire (pp. 48–49), which warms a known amount of water. The temperature rise of the water over a certain time, compared to the electric current passed through the wire, shows the relationship between the two. Joule's law states that the heat produced is proportional to the resistance of the wire, the time the current flows, and the square of the current. His work was a further stage in the development of electricity as another branch of science.

Thermometer measures temperature rise

ELECTRICITY AND HEAT
The work of Englishman James Joule (1818–89) was dominated by his study of the connections between heat, electricity, and mechanical work. Joule showed that electricity and mechanical work did not just move heat from one place to another, as was believed at the time; they generated heat. Heat could also be turned into mechanical work. Joule's work was the basis of the modern concept of energy. A modern unit of energy, the "joule", is named after him.

Coiled resistance wire

Measured volume of water

Compass needle

Terminals for connection to electricity

Loop of wire carries current

THE GALVANOMETER
Joule used a tangent galvanometer in his experiments. Current flowing in the loop of wire produces a magnetic field. When the meter is set up correctly, the field deflects a small magnetic needle from its normal north-south alignment with the Earth's magnetic field. The current is proportional to the amount the needle is deflected from its original ("at rest") position.

INVENTION OF THE GALVANOMETER
Leopold Nobili (1784–1835) devised one of the earliest sensitive electrical measuring instruments, the astatic galvanometer (pp. 34–35). The galvanometer indicated current – the quantity of charge moving past a certain point per unit of time. In the 19th century, electric current produced by batteries was called galvanic current after Galvani (pp. 16–17).

AN AMMETER
By 1890 the expanding electricity business brough[t] the need for portable, accura[te] robust meters. This moving co[il] meter showed t[he] current in amps.

Flowing currents

Electricity has been likened to a fluid, flowing unseen from place to place. Some of the words used to describe electricity, such as "current" and "flow", relate to these notions. The comparison between electricity passing along wires and water flowing through pipes is not an exact parallel, but it can help to explain some of electricity's stranger properties by making them more physical and familiar.

WATER ANALOGY

The rate of water flow (the volume passing a certain point in a given time) is similar to the current in an electrical circuit, measured in amps. The pressure, or pushing force, of the water can be thought of as the potential difference in an electrical circuit, measured in volts. A narrower pipe resists water flow, as thin wire in a circuit resists the flow of electricity.

Flow meter shows two units of flow in this part of the circuit, where the water flow is slowed down because it had to turn the propellor

THE PROPELLOR

The propellor turns when the water flows by it. It resists the flow of water and this results in a slower flow, and a reduction in the number of units shown on the meter.

Propellor

RESISTANCE TO FLOW

Certain factors set up a resistance to flow (pp. 22–23). The propellor and the coils of tubing do this in the circuit shown here. The flow meters show less flow or current in their branches of the circuit, but the flows add up to the total flow from the pump. In electricity, resistance to the current could be provided by an electric motor or a conducting wire.

Flow meter shows one unit of flow in this part of the circuit, where there is resistance to flow set up by the long, thin pipe

METERS

Meters show the units of flow in the pipes, and they register how these units are shared between the parallel pipes in the circuit. In electricity these would be ammeters, measuring the current in amps.

POWER SOURCE

The pump represents the battery or other electricity source which provides the "pushing power", or pressure, to force the water through the pipes. In electricity this is measured by the voltage.

A resistance coil is made up of a long length of thin piping wound into a coil to make it more manageable in the circuit

Flow meter shows three units of flow as the water is pushed around the circuit by the pump

Pump provides the pushing power

Water flows in anti-clockwise direction

THE INTERNATIONAL VISUAL LANGUAGE OF ELECTRICITY

It would be time-consuming if all the information about electricity was written out in full. So symbols are used as an international visual language that is understood by electrical engineers, circuit designers, and teachers.

A = ampere/amp (p. 27)	J = joule (p. 24)
a.c. = alternating current (pp. 40–41)	kWh = kilowatt-hour (p. 46)
C = coulomb (p. 11)	p.d. = potential difference (p. 22)
d.c. = direct current (pp. 40–41)	V = volt (pp. 20–21)
e.m.f. = electromotive force (pp. 34–35)	W = watt (p. 42)
F = farad (p. 13)	Ω = ohm (pp. 22–23)
H = henry (p. 35)	

- a.c. supply (pp. 40–41)
- ammeter (pp. 22–23)
- battery (pp. 18–19)
- cell (pp. 16–19)
- fuse (p. 48)
- relay (pp. 30–31)
- resistor (pp. 22–23)
- switch (pp. 46–49)
- transformer (pp. 40–41)
- voltmeter

Magnetism from electricity

With the development of Volta's battery in 1800, scientists had a source of steadily flowing electric current. This opened up new fields of research. Twenty years later an observation by Hans Christian Oersted (1777–1851) from Copenhagen began to link the two great scientific mysteries of the age: electricity and magnetism. Oersted noticed that a metal wire carrying a current affected a magnetic compass needle that was brought near to it. This revelation, which contradicted orthodox philosophy of the time, was published in scientific journals. French scientific thinker André-Marie Ampère (1775–1836) heard about Oersted's work from a fellow scientist. He doubted it at first, so he repeated the tests, but had similar results. Ampère therefore set to work to describe the effect more fully and to explain the connection between electricity and magnetism. In repeating the experiments, he provided a theoretical and mathematical description of the practical results of Oersted's work. From this flowed discoveries such as the electromagnet (pp. 28–29) and the telegraph receiver (pp. 56–57).

OERSTED'S ANNOUNCEMENT
Oersted published his discovery of the interaction between electricity and magnetism on 21 July 1820. The pamph was written in Latin but was translated into various languages includir his own, Danish. Michael Faraday (pp. 34–35) would probably have heard about the discovery this way.

Current off

With no current in the wire, the filings lie haphazardly

Current on

THE MAGNETIC FIELD
Magnetism, like electricity, is invisible – but its effects can be seen. Iron-containing substances such as iron filings are attracted to an ordinary bar magnet, and they line up to indicate the direction of the invisible "lines of force" of the magnetic field. An electric current also creates a magnetic field. With no current in the wire, the filings lie randomly on the card. Switch the current on, tap the card, and the filings line up to reveal a circular magnetic field around the wire.

Filings line up indicating circular magnetic field

Trough battery

Battery terminal

Wooden clamp

Current-carrying wire

Dilute acid between plates

AMPÈRE'S ACHIEVEMENT

Ampère developed the science of electrodynamics. He proved that the strength of the magnetic field around a wire, shown by the amount of the compass needle's deflection, rises with increasing current, and decreases with the distance away from the wire. Ampère extended Oersted's work, but he could not see a clear relationship between the needle's movements and the position of the wire. Then he realized that the direction in which the needle settled depended on the Earth's magnetic field as well as the magnetic field produced by the current. He devised a way of neutralizing the Earth's magnetic field, and found that the needle then settled in the direction of the magnetic field produced by the current and not with the Earth's north-south magnetic field. Ampère also found that two parallel electric currents had an effect on each other. If the currents run in the same direction, they attract each other; if they run in opposite directions, they repel each other. To commemorate Ampère's achievements, the modern unit of current – the ampere (shortened to "amp") – was named after him.

André-Marie Ampère

Thumb points in the direction of movement

First finger points in the direction of the magnetic field

Second finger indicates flow of current

THE LEFT-HAND RULE

When an electric current crosses a magnetic field, then the magnetic field, the current, and the force on the current – and thus the movement of the wire carrying the current, if it can move (pp. 38–39) – are all in different directions. A current-carrying wire or other conductor in a magnetic field tries to move according to this handy rule. With the thumb and first two fingers of the left hand at right angles to each other, the first finger shows the direction of the magnetic field (points from the north pole to the south pole of the magnet); the second finger shows the flow of the electric current (points from positive to negative); and the thumb shows the movement of the wire.

Reconstruction of Oersted's experiment

Needle deflected from north-south by magnetic field of current in wire

Wooden clamp

South

North

Current-carrying wire

Current on

Current off

Needle aligns with Earth's north-south magnetic field

Hans Christian Oersted

THE PROCESS OF DEDUCTION

During a lecture in Copenhagen on changing electricity to heat, Oersted moved a compass near to the current-carrying wire. The wire caused the compass needle – which is a magnet – to swing away from its normal north-south alignment with the Earth's magnetic field. In this reconstruction of his demonstration, the stands and the bench are made from an insulating material so as not to disturb the magnetic field. Oersted had shown that magnetism had been produced by the electric current and this phenomenon is known as electromagnetism. Oersted's discovery became the basis of the electric motor (pp. 38–39) and the electromagnet (pp. 28–29), which is involved in many areas of our daily lives from music system loudspeakers to the starting of a car (pp. 30–31).

Plates of copper and zinc soldered back-to-back and cemented into wooden trough

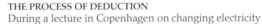

Electromagnets

THE DISCOVERY OF a magnetic field around a current-carrying wire (pp. 26–27), and the fact that a coil of wire had a greater magnetic effect than a single turn, led to a fascinating new gadget that made lecture audiences gasp with surprise. In 1825 William Sturgeon (1783–1850) wound a coil of wire around an iron rod and built one of the first electromagnets. An electromagnet differs from the usual permanent magnet – its magnetism can be turned on and off.

It usually consists of insulated electrical wire wound around a piece of iron, known as the core. Switch on the current, and the magnetic field around the wire makes the core behave as a magnet. It attracts iron-containing substances in the usual way. Switch off the electricity, and the magnetism disappears. Sturgeon built the electromagnets as demonstration models for his lectures.

ELECTROMAGNETIC CHAIR
A chair was a convenient base for this great horseshoe electromagnet of Michael Faraday (pp. 34–35). It was used to investigate the effects of magnetism.

Electromagnet with current off

Positive terminal to source of current

Negative terminal to source of current

Horseshoe-shaped core of soft iron

Wire connecting the two coils

Copper wire insulated with lacquer

With current off, there is no magnetism

Fabric insulation on iron core

Coil of wire

Sturgeon's electromagnet

Iron core

End connected to battery

STURGEON'S ELECTROMAGNET
Sturgeon was a craftsman and instrument maker who published catalogues of his electromagnetic apparatus (left). He enjoyed the practical "how-to" side of science, but had less concern for theories about why things happened. His electromagnet (above) depended on current passing through a coil of wire, to create an appreciable magnetic field. In his time, wires were made bare and uninsulated. He insulated the iron core to stop the electricity passing straight along it instead. (Later electromagnets had insulated wire.) The turns of the coil were also spaced apart, to prevent the current jumping straight from one to the next where they touched – short-circuiting.

End connected to battery

INVISIBLE LIFTING POWER
This modern electromagnet demonstrates its strength by attracting a loose pile of iron filings when the current is switched on. In a bar-shaped electromagnet, one end of the core becomes the north pole and the other is the south pole, depending on the current's direction of flow. This horseshoe-shaped core has two coils for a stronger magnetic field between its ends (bringing the poles closer together makes the magnet more powerful). Sturgeon made an initial discovery that soft iron was a good metal for the core, since it became magnetized more easily than steel. In the early days, there were races to build the biggest electromagnets and lift the heaviest weights. By the late 1820s electromagnets in Europe could lift around 5 kg (11 lb). In the United States, Joseph Henry realized that more turns in the coil produced a stronger magnetic field (up to a limit). It is said that he made insulated wire by wrapping bare wire with strips of silk from his wife's clothes. He could then pack more turns of wire into a smaller space, without the risk of short-circuit. The greater the current, the more powerful was the magnetic field. Henry's "Albany" electromagnet (opposite) lifted about 340 kg (750 lb).

Iron filings

Electromagnet with current on

Positive terminal to source of current

Negative terminal to source of current

Horseshoe-shaped core of soft iron

Wire connecting the two coils

Copper wire insulated with lacquer

...ce of ...gnetic field ...rcomes ...vity and ... iron ...gs

Henry's electromagnet

Non-magnetic stand

Iron core

Several layers of insulated wire

Zinc plate

Copper plate

Wooden base

JOSEPH HENRY
Henry (1797–1878) was an engineer whose inventive genius led him to improve electromagnets, for example by wrapping a second coil of wire around the first. In this small electromagnet (left), the two metal plates of copper and zinc were immersed in a jar of dilute acid. This formed a voltaic cell (pp. 16–17) that produced the electric current. The wire was wrapped in insulating fabric, so that the coil's turns could be close together for a stronger magnetic field. Henry also developed an early form of telegraph in 1831, although others made fame and fortune from it (pp. 56–57), and some of his work with electromagnetic induction paralleled that of Faraday.

HENRY'S LIFTING RIG
This type of apparatus was used to measure the lifting power of electromagnets made to different designs, from various metals, and with different numbers and arrangements of windings.

ELECTROMAGNETS AT WORK
The lifting power of modern electromagnets is used to separate iron-containing, or ferrous, metals from other materials at the scrapyard, before recycling.

Electromagnets at work

SINCE THE TIME OF STURGEON AND HENRY, electromagnets have been central components in electrical machines. Their power to attract and hold iron-containing materials, for example, when sorting out steel cans from aluminium ones at the recycling centre, is not their only use. An electromagnet is a convenient way of turning electrical energy into rotary motion, using the forces of magnetic attraction and repulsion in electric motors (pp. 38–39). The reverse occurs in generators (pp. 36–37). Electricity is converted into push-pull movements by electromagnetic relays and solenoids. The movements operate mechanical devices, such as telegraph receivers. Electro-magnetism is also used in electrical transformers (pp. 40–41), and to manipulate atoms in particle accelerators.

SAVING SIGHT
A finely controlled electromagnet could remove iron-containing foreign particles from the tissues of the eye. It pulled fragments straight out, minimizing the risk of further damage.

RINGING A BELL
Pressing the button of this doorbell completes a circuit in which the current passes into one terminal of the doorbell, then through the coil, the electromagnets, along the springy steel contact, into the brass screw and its mounting, and out through the other terminal. As the armature is pulled towards the electromagnets, the hammer hits the gong. At the same time, a gap opens between the contact spring and the screw, which breaks the circuit and switches off the electricity. The magnetism disappears, the spring on which the armature is mounted moves the armature back into its original position, the contacts touch and make the circuit again. The process is repeated until the button is released.

Gong

Hammer

Contact points

Contact-adjusting brass screw

Steel contact spring

Soft iron armature

Electromagnet

Spring mounting for armature

How a doorbell works

Hammer hits gong

Armature is pulled towards electro-magnets

Gap opens between contact spring and screw

Current passes to contact spring

Wires to doorbell button and electricity

THE DOORBELL
When the current is switched on, the electromagnet attracts a nearby piece of iron. The movement of the iron, known as the armature, can be used to switch on a separate electrical circuit. In this doorbell the armature also switches off its own circuit. Huge rows of relays are still the basis for some telephone exchanges (pp. 58–59).

ss ink bath — Tape drive roller — Clockwork motor

Return spring

Pivot rotates and feeds
paper past inking wheel

Iron bar

Terminals

Galvanometer for
testing purposes

Clockwork
winding
ey

pe emerges
om drawer
ntaining paper reel

Message-sending key

Electromagnet

TTING THE MESSAGE

s telegraphic receiver printed the dots and dashes
Morse code (pp. 56–57) on to paper tape. The tape was
ed by a roller driven by the clockwork motor. As an electric
rent flowed along the telegraph line, it energized the twin electromagnets.
ese attracted the iron bar, operating a system of levers, which pressed the
e against an inking wheel. When the current ceased, the return spring pulled
tape away from the inking wheel. The tape moved at a constant speed. A short burst
urrent inked a short line – the "dot"; a pulse three times as long made the "dash".

eparate parts of a starter solenoid

Casing contains wire coil
and heavy duty contacts

Iron plunger

Heavy duty
wires to
starter motor

Mounting bracket

RTING UP

olenoid is a cylindrical coil of wire, usually with an
core or plunger inside. At rest, the plunger sticks
of the coil. When the current is switched on, the
nger is attracted into the magnetic field created
de the coil, and pulled strongly into the middle
he coil. In a car the key-operated ignition
tch completes a circuit and energizes
starter solenoid. The iron
nger moves and closes
itch that completes a
arate circuit through
starter motor, which
s the engine. This
aration is necessary
ause a starter
tor draws a high
rent from the car's
ery which would
erwise deliver a
ck to the driver.

Ignition key
switches on
small current

Low-current circuit

Car battery

Plunger

Heavy duty
contacts

Motor is
activated

Starter
solenoid is
energized

Starter motor receives high current

ATOMIC PARTICLES
The study of sub-atomic
particles involves
accelerating them
to incredible speeds
(pp. 12–13). A magnetic
field deflects charged
particles, so powerful
electromagnets can be
adjusted to control, bend,
and focus their paths.
The Large Hadron
Collider seen here is
the world's largest and
highest-energy particle
accelerator, spanning
the border between
Switzerland and France.

Discoveries using electricity

In 1800 a few weeks after Volta announced his electricity-making pile (pp. 16–17), William Nicholson (1753–1815) and Anthony Carlisle (1768–1840) were experimenting with their own version. They noticed bubbles appearing in a drop of water on top of the pile. They then passed the electric current through a bowl of water. Bubbles of gas appeared around the two metal contacts where they dipped into the water. The bubbles around one contact were hydrogen, and the others were oxygen. The electric current had produced a chemical reaction, splitting water into its two elements. This was electrolysis. Soon other substances were being investigated. Humphry Davy brought electrolysis to prominence when he used it to make pure potassium and sodium for the first time. Today's uses include electroplating, refining pure copper, extracting aluminium from its treated natural ores, and making substances such as chlorine.

HUMPHRY DAVY
In 1807 Davy (1778–1829) made pure potassium by electrolysis. With a bigger electric current (p. 19), he made pure sodium. He helped popularize science, demonstrating such wonders as the intense light of an arc lamp (p. 37).

Battery as source of current

Current-carrying wires

Potash melted by current

MAKING PURE POTASSIUM FOR THE FIRST TIME
Pure potassium is a soft, silvery-white metal. It does not occur on its own in nature, because it combines so readily with other substances to form compounds. One is potash (potassium carbonate) found in the ashes of burned plants. This is an ingredient in certain types of glass. Davy passed a large current through molten potash in a metal pot, and pure potassium collected around the negative contact. He named the new substance potassium after its source. In the same way he prepared sodium from soda (sodium carbonate). Davy's successor at the Royal Institution, Michael Faraday, also studied electrolysis. Two laws of electrolysis are named after him.

Potassium reacts with air, so must be sealed

Pure potassium in a sealed glass tube

Modern
voltameter

*Electrolyte
(water with a
little sulphuric
acid) is poured
in here*

*Rising bubbles
of oxygen gas*

*Gases
drawn off
through
taps*

*Positive
electrode
(anode)*

*The gases
bubble
upwards*

*Positive
ions are
attracted
to the
negative
electrode*

Stand and supports

Connecting wire

*Negative
ions are
attracted to
the positive
electrode*

To electricity supply

ELECTROLYSIS IN ACTION
Only substances that conduct
electricity can be electrolysed.
The substance to be split is
called the electrolyte. Electricity
is passed through it between
two metal electrodes. In an
electrolyte, the molecules are
split into substances that
Faraday called positive and
negative ions. The positive ions
are attracted to the cathode and
the negative ions to the anode.
The electrical energy causes
chemical reactions in which the
ions gain or lose electrons.

Electroplating

In this process, an object receives a coating of a metal
by electrolysis. The object to be plated is connected to the
negative terminal of a battery or similar electricity supply
so that it acts as the negative electrode (cathode). It is left
for a time in a solution containing a compound of the
metal that will form the plating. For example, an
object to be plated with copper is put into
copper sulphate solution. This solution is
the electrolyte. In it, the copper exists as
positively charged ions. When the
electric current flows, these ions
are attracted to the negative
electrode – the object. They
settle evenly on its surface.

Nickel spoon

Silver plated spoon

**ELECTROPLATING
A SILVER SPOON**
Solid silver cutlery is
expensive, so cutlery
is often made from a
cheaper metal and thinly plated
with silver by electrolysis. The item must
be clean, otherwise the silver will not
adhere to its surface. Silver is transferred
from the solution to the object.

*Electroplating
tank*

*Electricity
supply*

*Spoon cathode
slowly revolves
to ensure even
plating*

*Silver
nitrate
solution*

*Silver
anode*

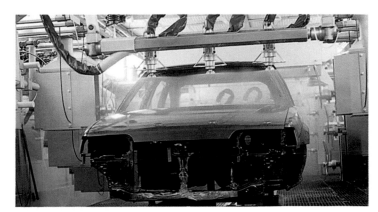

RUST-RESISTANT CARS
Steel vehicle bodies can be electroplated with a thin layer of a metal
such as zinc to protect them from rust. The car body (the cathode)
is electrified, and the zinc (the anode) is drawn from the solution
to cover every nook and cranny.

Electricity from magnetism

FATHER OF ELECTRICITY
Michael Faraday (1791–1867) studied many areas of science, including the effects of intense magnetism on light. This phenomenon led him to ideas that were to form the foundation of electromagnetic field theory (pp. 60–61).

WHEN AN ELECTRIC GUITARIST plucks a string in a vast stadium, the metal string is almost silent. However, its vibrations are detected by an electromagnetic pick-up, boosted by the amplifiers, and this fills the stadium with sound. The guitar's pick-up is one of the hundreds of electrical devices, including generators and transformers, that rely on electromagnetic induction – manipulating magnetism to make electricity. The principle was demonstrated in 1831 by Michael Faraday in Britain and by Joseph Henry in the United States. In electromagnetic induction, a varying or moving magnetic field produces an electromotive force (e.m.f.) in a nearby conductor, and thus an electric current if the conductor is part of a circuit (p. 20). The current flows only while the magnetic field varies.

Magnet

Coil

First coil conne to battery

Galvanometer

Swing of pointer indicates induced current

Thumb shows the direction of motion

First finger points in the direction of magnetic field

First finger points in the direction of magnetic field

Second finger points in the direction of the e.m.f.

MAGNET AND COIL
A wire can be subjected to a changing magnetic field by moving a nearby permanent magnet (above), or the changing magnetic field may come from an electromagnet (above right). In one of Faraday's experiments, a rod-shaped permanent magnet was thrust in and out of a coil of wire. The magnet was surrounded by invisible "lines of magnetic force", as might be traced out by iron filings (pp. 26–27). If the magnet is still, there is no change in the magnetic field, and no current flows. When the magnet moves, its lines of force cross the wire and so induce a current, which can be detected by a galvanometer (p. 24). The idea of "lines of magnetic force" was one of many proposed by Faraday.

RIGHT-HAND RULE
This useful rule helps work out the direction of the induced current. It relates the direction of the magnetic field (north to south), the direction of movement in a generator, and the e.m.f. or current (positive to negative). The direction of movement in an electric motor is shown by the left-hand rule (p. 27).

FARADAY'S INDUCTION RING
Faraday investigated the effects of electromagnetic induction using this equipment (left). One wire is wound in a coil around part of an iron ring, with ends to connect to the terminals of a battery. A separate wire is wound around another part of the ring – it does not touch the first wire. Its ends are connected to a galvanometer. When the first coil is connected to the battery, a magnetic field builds up almost instantaneously around it, and in the iron ring. As the magnetic field forms, it induces a current in the second coil, which shows as a sudden swing of the galvanometer pointer. In a split second the magnetic field has formed and becomes steady, so current no longer flows. If the first coil is disconnected from the battery, the magnetic field collapses, again inducing a pulse of electric current in the second coil, but in the other direction.

Galvanometer shows existence of current

Second coil connected to galvanometer

Soft iron ring

RECORD KEEPING
An entry in Faraday's notebook, dated 29 August 1831, shows his sketch of the induction ring apparatus. Faraday always kept careful scientific records.

...s to hold mercury to improve ...ctrical connections

Terminals

Fabric insulation

CONTINUOUS MOVEMENT
This 1870s model of a disc generator demonstrates one of Faraday's experiments of 1831. An e.m.f. (voltage) is induced in the copper disc when it is rotated in the magnetic field between the poles of the electromagnet. Spring contacts on the edge of the disc and the axle connect to terminals on the base. If a galvanometer is connected to these terminals, the circuit will be completed and a current will flow.

Electromagnet creates strong magnetic field

Axle

...per ... ...t into ...al ...e

...RY'S INDUCTION COIL
...g a coil of copper strips, Joseph Henry recognized another ...t known as self-inductance. He discovered that a wire carrying ...anging current not only induces a voltage in nearby conductors, ...also in itself. This makes it impossible to start and stop a current ...ntaneously. The unit of electrical inductance is called the henry.

Hand crank turns the disc

Copper disc turns in the magnetic field

Terminal

Spring contact

1889-26

Magneto-electric machines

THE RESEARCHES of Henry, Faraday, and others in the 1830s were followed gradually by practical machines that converted mechanical energy to electrical energy. These machines were known as magneto-electric machines. Later they used electro-magnets and came to be called generators or dynamos. The earliest uses were as demonstration models and for medical treatment (pp. 50–51). Electroplating (pp. 32–33) was the earliest serious application in 1844, followed by lighthouse illumination. It was not until the 1880s that innovations in design led to their use for electric lighting (pp. 42–43).

CLARKE'S MACHINE
Edward Clarke, a London instrument maker, designed an efficient magneto-electric machine where turning the handle rotated coils of wire, not a large magnet as in Pixii's machine (right). Clarke's machine was used for demonstrations and medical treatments (pp. 50–51).

Wooden frame

Iron core

Wire coil

Wire coil

North pole of rotating permanent magnet

South pole of rotating permanent magnet

Wire connecting coil to commutator

Commutator

Hand-turned wheel

Commutator contact

PIXII'S MACHINE
In 1832 Hippolyte Pi devised a hand-crank "magneto-electric machine" to produce electricity. A set of gears turned a large horseshoe-shaped permanent magnet, close to two coils of wire linked into a circuit. The source energy was the opera turning the crank. Th magnets were always turned in the same direction, but the line of force which made the magnetic field w in one direction whe the north pole of the magnet moved past a coil and in the othe direction when the south pole moved pa the coil. This induce an alternating electri current in the circuit For the convenience of having a one-way current, Pixii incorporated a commutator on his machine.

Coil of
electromagnet

Coil of
electromagnet

Magnet pole

Armature

Drive pulley

Wire gauze
brush

Commutator

Wire gauze
brush

Magnet pole

GRAMME DYNAMO

In about 1870 Belgian inventor
Z T Gramme devised a dynamo that
generated enough electric current,
flowing sufficiently steadily, to be
useful for large-scale applications,
such as illuminating factories by
carbon arc lights (below). The
rotating part of the dynamo, bearing
the coils of wire, is known as the
armature. Gramme's dynamos were
steam-driven and, unlike their
predecessors, did not overheat in
continuous operation. The Gramme
dynamo produced a one-way or
direct current (d.c.). It incorporated
a commutator – segments of copper,
which rotated with the armature and
caused the current to flow in one
direction only. Wire gauze brushes
rubbing against the commutator
picked up the current. The dynamo
was expensive to maintain because
the commutator and brush contacts
became worn by pressure and the
sparks that flew between them.

Arc lamp

Electro-
magnetic
mechanism

WERNER VON SIEMENS

The German Siemens family
made many contributions to
electrical engineering. Werner
von Siemens (1816–92)
designed a dynamo (1866) that
used opposing electromagnets
to produce a magnetic field
around the armature, rather
than around a permanent
magnet (p. 36).

Carbon rods for lighting

An early use for dynamo-generated electricity was
arc lighting. The arc is a "continuous spark" between
carbon rods – carbon being a good conductor
(p. 21). Arc lamps threw intense light, but they
were inefficient, unpredictable, and needed
constant attention. Even so, they were installed in
lighthouses, public buildings, and street lighting.

PUBLIC LIGHTING

In an arc lamp, the
gap between the
carbon rods is
critical. It needs
regular adjustment
because the gap
widens as the
carbon vaporizes. A
mechanism operated
by electromagnets
controls the upper
carbon rod to keep
the necessary gap.

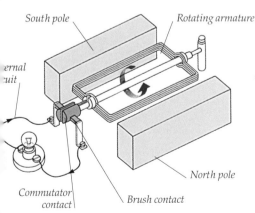

South pole

Rotating armature

External
circuit

Commutator
contact

Brush contact

North pole

HOW THE DYNAMO WORKS

A coil of wire (the armature) is rotated between
the poles of permanent magnets. As one side
of the coil travels past the north pole, it cuts the
lines of magnetic force, and a current is induced.
The coil moves on and the current dies away. Then
it approaches the south pole, inducing a current in
the opposite direction. The coil is attached to the
commutator which causes the current on the external
circuit to flow in the same direction all the time.

HOW THE ARC WORKS

The electric current passes
through the pointed tips
of the rods as they touch.
It heats them so much
that the carbon vaporizes.
As the rods are drawn apart,
the vapour will carry the
current across the small
gap, glowing intensely as it
does so. Davy and Faraday
demonstrated arcs at their
lectures (pp. 34–35).

19th-century lighthouses at La
Hève, France, which used arc lamps

Carbon
rod

Carbon
rod

Gap
where
white
light is
produced

Making things move

Iɴ 1821, ᴛʜᴇ ʏᴇᴀʀ ᴀꜰᴛᴇʀ Oᴇʀsᴛᴇᴅ's ᴅɪsᴄᴏᴠᴇʀʏ of a connection between electricity and magnetism (pp. 26–27), Michael Faraday devised a simple apparatus in which a current-carrying wire rotated around a magnetic pole. It was the first electric motor, although it was too crude to have any practical use. During the 1830s many types of primitive electric motors were built, and some were used to drive machines. The American engineer Thomas Davenport used them to turn a drill and lathe, but they were inefficient and expensive, partly because the source of electricity to drive them was a battery. By the 1870s dynamos (p. 37) were able to provide a cheaper source of electricity, and engineers had learned that when a dynamo operated in reverse and was supplied with electric current, it made an efficient motor. The commercial use of motors grew, especially traction motors to drive trains.

Metal support arm carries current

Wire to battery

CONTINUOUS MOTION
In Faraday's "electro-magnetic rotation apparatus", electric current produced continuous movement. A stiff wire was suspended from a flexible one, so that it could move freely. The lower part of the stiff wire was placed near one pole of a permanent magnet. The end of the wire dipped into a dish of mercury (a metal that is liquid at normal room temperatures). The mercury allowed the end of the wire to move and, being a metal, it also conducted electricity. When a current flowed through the wire, this produced a magnetic field around it. The field interacted with the magnetic field around the magnet, and the wire began to move around it. The liquid mercury allowed the wire to rotate around the magnet, while still maintaining the circuit and permitting the current to flow.

BARLOW'S WHEEL
In this apparatus, devised by Peter Barlow (1776–1862) in 1823, a star-shaped metal wheel was free to rotate on an axle, within the magnetic field of a horseshoe magnet. Current flowing from a battery through the wheel set up a magnetic field around it, and so the points of the star near the horseshoe magnet moved. The points of the wheel dipped into a mercury bath below, to maintain the circuit while allowing the wheel to move.

ELECTROMAGNETIC ROTATIO
In a drawing of one of Farada versions, a wire rotated aroun magnet (right), while in anotl (left), the magnet rotated arou a fixed wi

Rotating conductor

Bar magnet

Liquid mercury

Wire to battery

Glass dish

ELECTROMAGNETIC ENGINE

[Th]is 1835 model was typical of the [en]gines of the time in that it used [rec]iprocating motion like pistons [in] the cylinder of a steam engine [p. 42]). These engines were not [suc]cessful because they reflected [con]temporary steam engine [tech]nology which was [ina]ppropriate for electricity.

Hinged arm is drawn down

Iron bar

Wheel turns

Small arm is pulled down

Electromagnets attract iron bar

[H]OW THE MOTOR WORKS

[In] a simple electric motor, current [flo]ws through a coil of wire (the [ar]mature) between the poles of a [pe]rmanent magnet. When a current [flo]ws through any wire in a magnetic [fie]ld, there is a force on it (p. 27). [Th]e forces on the coil push one side [of] it down and the other side up. The [co]mmutator (p. 37) on the end of [th]e rotating shaft reverses the direction [of] the current through the coil twice [ev]ery revolution, which keeps the [coi]l rotating in the same direction.

South pole

Rotating coil of armature

Battery

Commutator

Brush contacts

North pole

THE ELECTRIC TRAIN

In the 1870s the Siemens company in Germany (p. 37) experimented with electric motors strong enough to pull a train. The Siemens electric railway was demonstrated at the Berlin Trade Exhibition in 1879.

EDISON'S ELECTRIC PEN

In 1880 this early commercial application of a small electric motor relied on current from a battery. The spinning motor operated a treadle system that made the needle inside the pen jab up and down 130 times each second. The needle point was used to perforate a stencil sheet, from which multiple copies could be made with an ink roller.

Close-up of 1930s sewing machine

Shaft

1930s sewing machine

[MO]TORS ENTER THE HOME

[Wh]en Isaac Singer produced his sewing machine [in 1]850, one breakthrough was the foot-operated [trea]dle, which left both hands free. In the 1930s [ano]ther new attachment appeared – an electric [mo]tor to work the needle and bobbin housing. [Th]e motor has outer electromagnets and a multi-coil [inn]er armature (p. 40). Small, powerful electric [mot]ors opened up a new world of tools and gadgets. [Com]pared to many other machines, the modern [elec]tric motor is extremely efficient. It turns more [tha]n 90 per cent of the energy fed into it, as [elec]tricity, into the energy of motion. Today, [man]y everyday appliances, from vacuum cleaners [to r]efrigerators, hairdryers and electric drills, use [elec]tric motors of one sort or another.

Coils of armature

Coils of electromagnet

Iron core

Electrical socket

Crank system to drive bobbin

Manipulating electricity

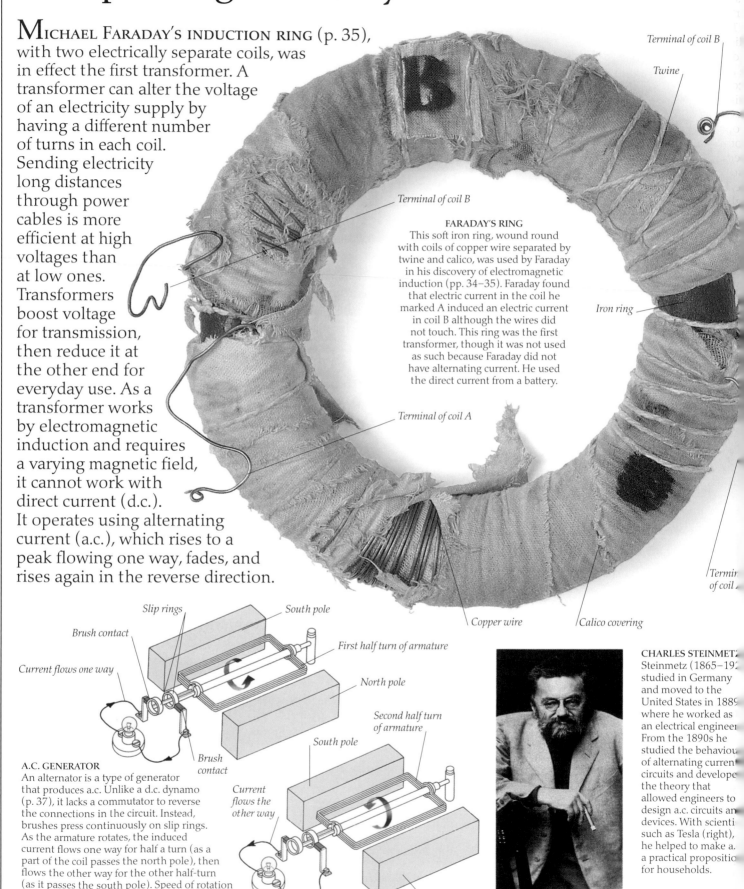

Michael Faraday's induction ring (p. 35), with two electrically separate coils, was in effect the first transformer. A transformer can alter the voltage of an electricity supply by having a different number of turns in each coil. Sending electricity long distances through power cables is more efficient at high voltages than at low ones. Transformers boost voltage for transmission, then reduce it at the other end for everyday use. As a transformer works by electromagnetic induction and requires a varying magnetic field, it cannot work with direct current (d.c.). It operates using alternating current (a.c.), which rises to a peak flowing one way, fades, and rises again in the reverse direction.

Terminal of coil B

Twine

Terminal of coil B

FARADAY'S RING
This soft iron ring, wound round with coils of copper wire separated by twine and calico, was used by Faraday in his discovery of electromagnetic induction (pp. 34–35). Faraday found that electric current in the coil he marked A induced an electric current in coil B although the wires did not touch. This ring was the first transformer, though it was not used as such because Faraday did not have alternating current. He used the direct current from a battery.

Iron ring

Terminal of coil A

Termin of coil A

Copper wire

Calico covering

A.C. GENERATOR
An alternator is a type of generator that produces a.c. Unlike a d.c. dynamo (p. 37), it lacks a commutator to reverse the connections in the circuit. Instead, brushes press continuously on slip rings. As the armature rotates, the induced current flows one way for half a turn (as a part of the coil passes the north pole), then flows the other way for the other half-turn (as it passes the south pole). Speed of rotation determines how quickly the current reverses.

Slip rings

Brush contact

South pole

Current flows one way

First half turn of armature

North pole

Brush contact

Second half turn of armature

South pole

Current flows the other way

North pole

CHARLES STEINMETZ
Steinmetz (1865–192
studied in Germany
and moved to the
United States in 1889
where he worked as
an electrical engineer
From the 1890s he
studied the behaviou
of alternating current
circuits and develope
the theory that
allowed engineers to
design a.c. circuits an
devices. With scienti
such as Tesla (right),
he helped to make a.
a practical propositio
for households.

Nikola Tesla

...sla (1856–1943), who was born in Croatia of ...rbian parents, emigrated to the United States ...1884. He worked briefly for Thomas ...ison. Several years earlier Tesla ...d realized how he could build ...a.c. motor that would not need ...commutator (p. 37). In 1888 he ...ilt his first "induction motor". This ...s a major factor in the widespread ...option of a.c. supplies. The induction ...otor is probably still the most widely ...ed type of electric motor today. Tesla ...o invented a type of transformer, ...e Tesla coil, which works at very ...gh frequencies and produces ...ormous voltages.

...UCTION MOTOR

...e induction motor has no brushes ...commutators. It uses a "rotating ...gnetic field", made by rapidly ...ding carefully timed alternating ...rents to a series of outer windings – ...stator – to produce a magnetic ...d pattern which rotates. The inner ...of windings on the shaft is the ...or. The stator's magnetic field ...uces a current in the rotor, and ...s becomes an electromagnet too. ...the stator's magnetic field pattern ...ates, it "drags" the rotor with it.

READING IN A THUNDERSTORM
Tesla imagined that one day even the power of lightning bolts could be harnessed. This photograph shows him reading at his high-voltage research laboratory in the United States in 1899, surrounded by giant sparks and bolts of electricity.

Stator winding

Brass frame

Rotor

Wooden base

Rotor shaft

Rods form part of brass frame

...nection to a.c. ...ricity supply

...PPING UP OR DOWN
...change of voltage in a transformer depends on the ...mber of turns in the two coils, called the primary and ...ondary windings. If the secondary has more turns than ...primary, voltage is increased (stepped up). If it has fewer, ...age is decreased (stepped down). There is no magical ...n – as voltage rises, ...ent falls, keeping ...overall electrical ...rgy the same.

Step-up transformer

Primary windings to electricity source

Secondary windings connected to high voltage lines

Step-down transformer

Primary windings to electricity source

Secondary windings connected to load – electric motors

TRANSFORMERS IN INDUSTRY
The generators at a modern power station do not produce electricity at sufficiently high voltage for efficient transmission. Their voltage is increased by step-up transformers for efficient long-distance transmission.

Early electricity supplies

THROUGH THE MID 19TH CENTURY visionaries attempted to put electricity to practical use and even replace steam power, but with no results apart from electroplating (p. 33), some instances of arc lighting (p. 37) and a few small models. In the 1860s efficient generators such as steam turbines were developed, and electricity became available on a larger scale. In the 1880s the rocketing demand for incandescent lamps (pp. 46–47) provided the stimulus for electricity distribution networks. At first, all electricity was generated at the place where it was to be used. This remained the case for a long while until the first central generating stations (pp. 43–45) were built and took over from the small, isolated units.

STEAM ENGINES
James Watt (1736–1819) was a Scottish engineer who made important improvements to the steam engine, thereby helping to stimulate the Industrial Revolution. The unit of power, the watt, is named after him. In electricity, the number of watts is obtained by multiplying volts by amps (p. 25).

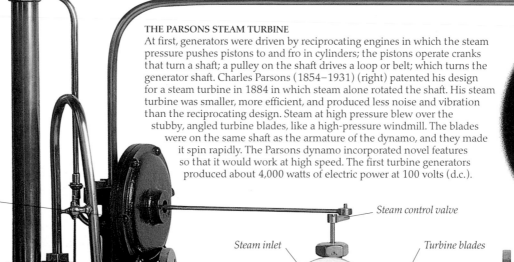

Pipe from governor to diaphragm

THE PARSONS STEAM TURBINE
At first, generators were driven by reciprocating engines in which the steam pressure pushes pistons to and fro in cylinders; the pistons operate cranks that turn a shaft; a pulley on the shaft drives a loop or belt; which turns the generator shaft. Charles Parsons (1854–1931) (right) patented his design for a steam turbine in 1884 in which steam alone rotated the shaft. His steam turbine was smaller, more efficient, and produced less noise and vibration than the reciprocating design. Steam at high pressure blew over the stubby, angled turbine blades, like a high-pressure windmill. The blades were on the same shaft as the armature of the dynamo, and they made it spin rapidly. The Parsons dynamo incorporated novel features so that it would work at high speed. The first turbine generators produced about 4,000 watts of electric power at 100 volts (d.c.).

Charles Parsons

Diaphragm

Steam control valve

Steam inlet

Turbine blades

Main shaft

Bearing to support shaft

Strong casing (cutaway)

Bearing to support shaft

Electromagr produces magnetic fie

ELECTRICITY FROM STEAM
Inside a steam generator, steam at pressure is fed through a central inlet into the turbine section, which consists of a spinning shaft inside a strong casing. Half the steam flows in each direction. It rushes through an array of alternate moving turbine blades, which it pushes around, and fixed guide vanes, which guide it in the most efficient way. As steam progresses, its pressure drops but the Parsons turbine distributes this drop in pressure along the blades. The long shaft has a 15-coil armature and commutator mounted near one end. The magnetic field around the armature is produced by the field coils – electromagnets on a horseshoe-shaped iron core.

Steam flows over the blades

Rotating blades spin armature

Armatu

How the steam turbine works

Electricity to the people

Thomas Edison (1847–1931) began his career as a telegrapher on North American railroads. He turned to inventing, developing things that people might want, which he could patent and sell. His first money-maker, in 1870, was an improved stock ticker. This device communicated stock and share prices telegraphically between offices in New York's financial area. There followed a string of inventions and improvements to other people's inventions. Edison was a central figure in the move towards large-scale distribution of electricity to factories, offices, and homes. One of his commercial aims was to break the monopoly of the gas companies, which he considered unfair.

Thomas Edison

Electrical control governor regulates steam pressure via pipe to diaphragm

Field coils – electromagnets on horseshoe-shaped core

Armature

Brush contact

Commutator

Bearing to support shaft

HORSE-DRAWN POWER
The early Parsons turbine generators could be moved by means of a horse-drawn cart to the required site. Their uses were varied. Some were used to provide temporary electric lighting. In 1886 this practical Parson's turbine was used to provide the electric light for ice skating after dark in the north-east of England when a local pond froze.

PEARL STREET PLANT
In 1882 Edison and his colleagues fitted steam boilers and improved dynamos into a building on Pearl Street, New York, shown here in this stylized engraving. He had cables installed to distribute the current to the surrounding city district south of Wall Street. Edison manufactured light bulbs and all the other components needed to make it easy for people to equip their homes for electric lighting.

CITY LIGHTS
Before incandescent lamps (p. 47), some city streets were lit by electric arc lamps, as in this New York scene of 1879. But the light was unpleasantly glaring and unreliable (p. 37), so gas was used for most street lighting.

The power station

An electricity supply is regarded as a major requirement for a modern "civilized" society. In the late 19th century electricity generating power stations were being installed in many of the world's large cities, although it was some decades before the suburbs, and then the rural areas, received supplies. Today, electricity is such a familiar and convenient form of energy that it is simply called "power" – a word with its own scientific meaning (the rate at which energy is used). The majority of modern power stations use turbines to turn generators. These turbines are turned by running water in hydroelectric power stations, or by steam obtained from water boiled by the heat from burning coal, oil, nuclear fuel, or some other source. Less-developed areas may obtain their electricity from local generators.

BIGGER AND BETTER
This model shows the planned Deptford Central Station of the London Electricity Supply Corporation. The engineer who designed it, Sebastian Ferranti (1864–1930), believed it would be more economical to build large power stations outside cities where land was cheap, and to transmit the power at high voltage to substations near the users. Unfortunately, he was ahead of his time. Bureaucracy and technical problems kept the station from being completed. The machines on the right-hand side were installed and supplied power. The enormous ones on the left were never finished.

Flat copper coils

Feedpipes

Flywheel

Connecting rod to crank shaft

Check valve

POWER FOR NEW YORK
Great power stations, such as this Edison Company station in New York, were often built on riverbanks or coastlines. The coal to fire the boilers could be delivered by barge, and river or sea water supplied the cooling requirements. Electricity changed people's lives, but smoke belched from the chimneys and soot settled over the neighbourhood.

DISTRIBUTION NETWORK
A typical power station generator produces alternating current at 25,000 volts. This is stepped up to hundreds of thousands of volts to reduce the energy loss during long-distance transmission. A main substation step-down transformer (pp. 40–41) reduces the voltage for the local area. Smaller substation transformers reduce it further for distribution to offices and homes.

Power station

Renewable energy

The production of electricity is using up non-renewable sources – coal, oil, and gas. Sustainable or renewable energy sources, that will not run out, are being used increasingly around the world for generation. They include rushing water in rivers as hydropower, the energy of moving air in wind turbines, and light from the Sun as solar power. Other sources are waves and tides, flammable gases from rotting plants, and heat from deep inside the Earth.

Dynamos (behind) are driven by 40 ropes direct from flywheel

Drive pulley or drum

linders

Combined engine and dynamos

hick concrete floor to support heavy machinery

Feedpipes from boiler

POWER FROM THE SUN
Solar panels contain many hundreds or thousands of units called photovoltaic (pv, "light-electricity") cells. Most standard cells are fingernail- to hand-sized and produce 0.5–2 volts of electricity. For best results the panels point at the midday sun. This photovoltaic power station is located in Paris, France.

HYDROELECTRIC POWER
Glen Canyon dam on the Colorado River in the United States channels running water through great turbines, which turn generators. In countries with sufficient rainfall and plentiful fast rivers, such as New Zealand, hydroelectric stations generate most of the total electricity needs.

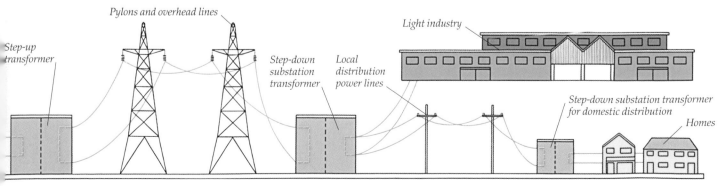

Pylons and overhead lines

Step-up transformer

Step-down substation transformer

Local distribution power lines

Light industry

Step-down substation transformer for domestic distribution

Homes

Electricity in the home

Electricity was first wired from power stations into homes, offices, and factories in the 1880s, in big cities such as New York, London, and Paris. Its first major use was for lighting – and it seemed both miraculous and mysterious. More convenient than gas lights, oil lamps, and candles, the flick of a switch could now transform night into day. In 1882 Thomas Edison's factories made 100,000 light bulbs, but because of the years it took to lay cables and establish electricity locally, electric light was not easily available until the 1930s. The new power was dangerously invisible. A wire looked the same, whether it was carrying a current or not. Early users were warned of the new dangers, though electricity was still safer than the naked flames of candles and gas.

THE MESSAGE
By 1900 demand for electric light bulbs in the United States was 45 million.

Early electric meter

ELECTRICITY METERS
An early meter (left), pioneered by Thomas Edison, used electrolysis (pp. 32–33) to measure the electricity used. The current passed through copper sulphate solution in the jars. The passage of the electric current caused the copper to dissolve on one plate and be deposited on the other. The change in weight of the plates was proportional to the electricity used. The wavy resistance wire and the lamp below prevented the solution from freezing in winter. By the 1930s the meter (below) had a spinning plate moved by induction (pp. 34–35), geared to a series of dials. These showed the amount of electric energy used, measured in kilowatt-hours (1,000 watts of power for one hour of time).

1930s meter

Jar containing copper sulphate solution

Resistance wire

Copper plates

Lamp to provide heat

Dials showing kilowatt hours

READING THE METER
Officials from electricity companies were soon visiting consumers on a regular basis to read the electricity meter. The meter reader switched off the supply, removed the copper plate, replaced it with a new one, and took the plate away for weighing. In this way the company worked out how much the consumer should pay.

Spinning plate moved by induction

lectric lamps

round 1880 light bulbs were developed
Edison, Joseph Swan (1828–1914), and
hers. These bulbs were called filament or
randescent bulbs, because of the way
y worked. Electricity flowed through a
n piece of carbon with high resistance –
e filament. This became so hot that it
wed white, or incandesced.
he filament glowed, oxygen in the air
uld combine with it and quickly burn it
ay. So air was sucked out of the bulb, to
ate a vacuum around the filament.

Filament light bulb

FILAMENT LAMP
filament light bulb works on the same
nciple as the Edison-Swan versions,
the materials have changed. The
nents made of tungsten can now
hstand very high temperatures. The
ment may be 50 cm (20 in) long,
coiled tightly to take up little
ce. An inert gas such as argon, to
uce evaporation of the tungsten,
replaced the vacuum.

son
w-in bulb

ntact
tal end

tal
ew
ing

rbonized
nboo
ment

uum
hin bulb

Bulb fits into ceramic safety cover

Wires carry electricity to and from filament

Filament support

Inert gas such as argon

*Hard metal
tungsten
filament*

*Wires carrying
electricity to
and from filament*

FLUORESCENCE
The French scientist Antoine
Becquerel (1852–1908) used
fluorescent light in his discovery
of radioactivity. This type of light
works when a substance gives
off light after being stimulated
by other rays, such as invisible
ultraviolet (UV) light. However,
practical fluorescent lamps were
not in use until the 1950s.

TURNING ON THE LIGHT
This early electrical switch has
the metal components in a ceramic
body. Two metal arms are sprung
so they flick quickly from one
position to another. When the
switch is turned on, the arms
slot into U-shaped springy
contacts, so completing the
electrical circuit. This must
happen fast, and the contacts
must be good, or the electricity
could spark across any gaps
and cause damage.

Switch turned on

*Sprung
metal arm*

*Glass
discharge tube*

Circuit completed

Switch turned off

Ceramic body

Circuit broken here

SAVING POWER
"Low-energy" bulbs or
compact fluorescent
lamps, CFLs, have
mostly replaced filament
bulbs. They use between
four and eight times less
electricity for the same
light output, which
comes from the
fluorescent coating
inside the tube, and
last between 10 and
20 times longer.

Electrical appliances

As soon as electricity was available in houses, people began to think up new uses for it. Although the early 20th century saw the invention and design of "labour-saving" appliances to make domestic life easier, the electric iron was the only appliance commonly found in the home, along with electric lights. Most early appliances used the ability of electricity to generate heat in appliances like hair curling tongs. When electric motors (pp. 38–39) came into wide use in the 1900s, electricity could be converted into movement. The range of appliances grew to include small heaters, food beaters, and hairdryers. However, the large appliances, such as the vacuum cleaner, were still only found in more affluent homes.

ELECTRIC COOKING
Still rare, electric cooking in the 19th century offered freedom from the smoke, burning coals, and hot ashes of the traditional stove. Hotplates could be switched on and off, and adjusted in temperature, to give the cook greater control.

Arc jumps here

Carbon rod

Insulated wire

Wooden handle

Connection for electric flex

Heavy cast-iron base

SMOOTHING IRON
The first electric irons used a high-temperature electric spark for a heat source. This was an arc, jumping between carbon rods. The rods burned away, so they had to be manually slid together when the electricity was turned off, to maintain the correct gap between them. Like the carbon arc lights, which used the same principle (p. 37), this method of changing electricity into heat was unsafe and unreliable. In 1883 the safety iron was patented in the United States. It replaced the carbon rods with a heating element.

Individual fuses   Indicator light

Lighting ring main

Power ring main

THE HOUSE MAINS
Most modern houses have different electrical circuits serving different needs. The basic circuits are for lighting fixtures and to carry electricity to the wall sockets. The power ring main usually has thicker cables, since it may have to supply appliances that require a high current. In some countries there is a separate heavy-duty circuit to provide electricity to the kitchen appliances.

Individual switches for plates

Wires carrying power to switchboard and cooker

Wires from switchboard to cooker encased in corrugated metal

Iron plate

High-resistance wire inside insulated cast-iron case

ELECTRIC COOKING
In this 1900 cooker, coils of high-resistance wire were placed beneath iron plates. The wire became hot as electricity flowed through it, and the heat passed to the plate. Insulating materials were necessary to prevent electricity flowing from the wire to the plate.

Copper reflecting dish

Wire safety grill

ELECTRIC KETTLE
Water and electricity are a dangerous combination, since water is an electrical conductor. The first electric kettles had a separate compartment for the element beneath the water. The element heated the container itself but most heat passed into the air. The Swan electric kettle of 1921 was the first with a fully insulated, waterproof heating element in the water.

Wooden handle

High-resistance coiled wire

Heating element

Copper body

Electric motor

Hinge to raise beaters

THE MOTORIZED BEATER
Mixing, whisking, and beating ingredients by hand is a tiring and time-consuming process. This 1918 food beater and mixer was one of the earliest to be driven by a small electric motor.

THE ELECTRIC PERCOLATOR
One of the chief advantages of an electrical appliance is that it can be moved around and used wherever there is a socket. This 1912 coffee maker is plugged in to an electric light socket.

Whisk

Supporting base for bowl

Current-carrying wire

ELECTRIC FIRE
The curly, high-resistance heating element in this 1930s portable heater glows a comforting red as electricity is pushed through it. The copper dish reflects the radiant heat. The types of wire used here show the principle of resistance (pp. 22–23); the high-resistance wire is used as the heating source because it glows hot while the insulated connecting wires that carry current stay cool and safe to the touch.

Electricity and medicine

THE WATERY SOLUTION OF CHEMICALS in living tissue makes a moderately good electrical conductor. Galvani noted the responses of dissected frog nerves and muscles to discharges from an electrostatic machine (p. 16), and many scientists detected electricity by the shocks it gave them. The body's own "electrical signals" are very small, measured in microvolts, and travel along nerves, sometimes at great speed. They detect, coordinate, and control, especially in the sense organs, brain, and muscles. If increasingly powerful electrical pulses are fed into the body, they cause tingling and then pain; they can send muscles into uncontrolled spasm, burn, render unconscious, and kill. However, doctors have discovered that, used carefully, electricity can diagnose, heal, and cure. Today, electrically heated scalpels slice and then seal small blood vessels to reduce bleeding during an operation. Controlled currents passing through tissue can relieve pain. Delicate surgery can be performed with electrical laser scalpels.

Horseshoe magnet

Terminal

Velvet-covered spinning coil

Tip that touches skin

A CURIOUS TREATMENT
This electro-medical machine of the 1850s had a handle and series of gear wheels which whirled coils of wire next to a horseshoe magnet, to generate electric current in the coils. A simple switch mechanism used this current and the self-inductance of the coils to produce a series of high-voltage pulses which caused an electric shock. The operator held the metal applicators by their insulating wooden handles, and applied the tips to the skin of the patient (below), so the pulses travelled through the tissues to treat rheumatism, headaches, and aching joints. When it was discharged through the patient's tissues, the shock often made the muscles contract uncontrollably.

EXECUTION
Movie villains sometimes meet their end in a dazzling flash of electricity. The reality is the electric chair, and the accidental electrocutions which occur each year in factories, offices, and homes as a result of carelessness.

Engraving showing the electro-medical machine in use

CONTROLLING ANIMALS
In the 19th century electricity was sometimes used for controlling vicious horses. A generator was operated by the driver to deliver a shock via a wire in the rein and the metal bit, into the horse's mouth.

ODDER'S ELECTRIC MACHINE

AUG. 1, 1854

Drive cord *Gear wheel*

Crank

THE ELECTROCARDIOGRAPH
Tiny "ripples" of electric current pass from working organs through the body's tissues to the skin. Here they can be detected by metal sensors and displayed as a wavy trace. A recording of the heart is an electrocardiogram, or ECG. The first ECG machine was developed in 1903 by Willem Einthoven (1860–1927). In this 1909 version (above) the patient is connected to the machine by placing one hand and one foot in bowls of conducting liquid.

Willem Einthoven

Implantable pacemaker (1962)

SETTING THE PACE
This pacemaker was the first implantable model. The heart's beating rate is set by its own pacemaker, a patch of tissue in the upper right-hand wall. This sometimes becomes faulty, or the electricity-conducting tissue that carries impulses through the heart muscle fails. An artificial pacemaker can be put under the skin and connected to the heart by a long wire (below).

Battery *Circuits*

Insulating wooden handles

Pacemaker implanted under skin

Electrode wire in jugular vein

tal bar trode

51

Heat, pressure, and light

ELECTRICITY CAN BE PRODUCED DIRECTLY from heat, pressure, and light. When heat is applied to one of the junctions of two conductors, so that the two junctions are at different temperatures, an electrical potential is generated; this is thermoelectricity. In the piezoelectric effect, an electrical potential is generated between opposite faces of crystals made from substances such as quartz, when the crystals are compressed – in simple terms, when the crystal is squeezed or stretched. In the photoelectric effect, light rays cause certain substances to give up electrons (p. 20) and produce an electric charge or current. In the photovoltaic effect, light produces an electrical potential between layers of different substances, so current flows in a circuit without need for an electricity source.

THOMAS SEEBECK
In the 1820s German scientist Thomas Seebeck (1770–1831) studied the effects of heat on conductors. This "Seebeck effect" is now known as thermoelectricity. There have been many attempts at using thermoelectricity. Its main use today is for thermometers (below right).

THE SEEBECK EFFECT
In a circuit of two metal strips joined at their ends, Seebeck heated the junction at one end and saw a compass needle between the strips swing. Seebeck thought the heat was creating magnetism. In fact an electric current was generated when the junctions were at different temperatures, and the magnetic field this produced deflected the compass needle. The Seebeck effect is effective only with certain conductors. Seebeck obtained his best results with the dissimilar conductors bismuth and antimony. A similar effect can be produced using iron and copper. The "opposite" is the Peltier effect, named after French scientist Jean Peltier (1785–1845). A temperature difference is produced between the junctions when an electric current from a battery flows round the circuit.

Reconstruction of Seebeck's experiment

Copper strip

Current flow around circuit

Junction at room temperature

Deflected compass needle

Junction being heated

Metal base

Iron strip

Bunsen burner

MAKING A THERMOCOUPLE
One application of the Seebeck effect is the type of thermometer based on a thermocouple (opposite). Above, the probe of the thermocouple is being made by welding a wire of platinum to a wire of platinum-rhodium alloy.

PIEZOELECTRIC EFFECT

In the crystal pickup of a record-player, mechanical vibrations produced in the stylus by the grooves in the record are transmitted to the piezoelectric crystal by a plastic stirrup. This produces a varying electrical signal to match the intended sound. The vibrations are directed in two directions, at right angles, to make the two channels necessary for stereophonic sound. The signal is amplified and then fed to loudspeakers (p. 61). Other applications of piezoelectricity include the audio bleeper and hand-squeezed spark-makers used for gas oven and burner lighters.

To amplifier for left channel

To amplifier for right channel

Quartz crystals inside case

Crystals produce voltage for amplification

Quartz crystals

Vibrations in stirrup transfer to quartz

Groove in vinyl record

Vibrations in stylus transfer to stirrup

LP·S ST 17D

Plastic stirrup

Stylus

PIERRE CURIE
The piezoelectric effect was first studied in about 1880 by Pierre Curie (1859–1906) and his brother Paul-Jacques (1856–1941). It is named from the Greek word *piezein* meaning to press. The Curies used Rochelle salt and quartz, natural crystals with piezoelectric qualities. Nowadays synthetic crystals are used.

Intensity of light produces voltage

Transparent gold layer

Connection to meter measuring current

PHOTOVOLTAIC CELL
This cell can be connected to a galvanometer (p. 24); the flowing current indicates the intensity of the light on the cell. This is the basis for one type of photographic exposure meter. The reading helps the photographer to determine the setting for the camera.

Connecting wire

digitherm

°C

Digital reading

Probe handle

PHOTOELECTRICITY IN SPACE
Like most spacecraft the Earth-orbiting Hubble Space Telescope, launched in 1990, needs electricity to operate. This comes from large wing-like solar panels or arrays that can swivel to point directly at the Sun. Hubble's panels have been replaced twice by Space Shuttle servicing missions, in 1993 and 2002. The newest panels produce 2,800 watts of electricity.

Probe tip

THERMOCOUPLE THERMOMETER
This device is based on the Seebeck effect. One junction of the thermocouple is at the tip of the probe. The thermocouple produces a voltage which depends on the difference between the temperature of this junction and the room temperature. The electronic circuitry in the display unit converts the voltage to a temperature difference, compensates for room temperature, and displays the result as a digital reading. This thermometer uses a nickel-chromium and nickel-aluminium thermocouple and measures temperatures from −50° C to 999° C (−58° F to 1830° F). Other types have a wider range. These thermometers have replaced the mercury type for many uses.

Investigating cathode rays

It was known in the 18th century that a gas at low pressure inside a tube could be made to glow by passing a discharge from an electrostatic machine through it. In the latter part of the 19th century new electrical apparatus enabled scientists to study the effect more thoroughly. For instance, improved vacuum pumps allowed the air pressure inside the tubes to be reduced. At very low pressures the glow disappeared, and was replaced by invisible rays which came from the cathode or negative terminal, and made the glass of the tube containing the gas glow green where the rays struck it. In 1883 Edison had noticed that particles seemed to be given off from the negative ends of the filaments of his electric light bulbs. The British scientist William Crookes was one of the discoverers of these "cathode rays". Later, J. J. Thomson extended this work with insights that led to the new science of atomic physics and to the discovery of the structure of the atom by Ernest Rutherford (1871–1937) and his team. The cathode ray tube became the basis for the television set (pp. 62–63) and radar equipment.

Replica of Crookes's tube

Cathode

Connection to low voltage

Tin Maltese cross

Anode

Shadow cast by cross

Connection to high voltage

WILLIAM CROOKES
An accomplished experimenter, Crookes (1832–1919) helped to found the science of spectroscopy and discovered thallium.

CROOKES'S EXPERIMENT
In the original apparatus (above) the electrons that formed the cathode rays were produced by a complex interaction between the cathode and the residual gas in the tube. In Crookes's famous experiment in 1887, a small metal cross shape was put in the path of the rays coming from the cathode. The cross cast a shadow on the glass screen beyond. This demonstrated that rays came from the cathode, and that they travelled in straight lines – just as a torch shining light rays on to the cross shape would cast a shadow behind it.

Crookes's Maltese cross experiment

Cathode

Anode made positive by connection to positive terminal

Shadow cast by cross on to end of tube

Front view of
modern apparatus

*Calibrations to
show deflection*

Thomson's tube

Vacuum tube

Anodes

*Metal plates
deflect electrons
electrostatically*

*Electromagnetic coils
deflect moving electrons*

Cathode

THE DISCOVERY OF THE ELECTRON

Joseph John Thomson (1856–1940) is credited with identifying the first subatomic particle, now called the electron, in 1897. Thomson knew that cathode rays could be "bent" or deflected by a magnetic field. He devised an experiment to measure the ratio of the charge carried by particles, which he believed made up cathode rays, to their mass. This involved balancing two separate forces on the particles, one produced by the magnetic field of the current flowing in a pair of coils, and the other by the electric field between two metal plates. Thomson explained his results by suggesting that cathode rays consisted of particles which carried an electric charge. This charge was equal to the charge carried by the hydrogen ions involved in electrolysis (p. 33). This proved that there was a particle even smaller than the hydrogen atom. He called it the electron.

J J Thomson

Fleming's tube

FLEMING'S TUBE

The Fleming tube, also called the thermionic valve or a vacuum tube, was invented by John Fleming (1849–1945) and patented in 1904. It was designed to detect the faint signals transmitted by Marconi's recently invented radio sets (pp. 60–61). A triode developed by Lee De Forest in 1906 (p. 61) was able to amplify radio signals. The cathode (negative electrode) was a hot wire that gave off electrons. These were attracted across the vacuum in the tube to the anode (positive electrode), but could not go the other way. Connected to an alternating voltage, the device thus allowed current to pass in one direction as a series of pulses. Through this capacity to amplify feeble electrical signals, the vacuum tube became the key to the development of all electronic machines.

Vacuum tube

Anode

*Hot
filament
acts as
cathode*

Supporting frame

Heated wire

ODERN DEMONSTRATION
odern apparatus
rons are produced more
y in larger quantity
a heated wire – the
t noticed by Edison
now called thermionic
sion. The anode is
a high positive voltage.
attracts the electrons
the cathode and
erates them. The
rons strike a fluorescent
on the inside of the
causing it to glow
tly – much more
tly than the plain
of the original tubes.

Low-voltage supply

High-voltage supply

*Terminal for
electricity supply*

Communicating with electricity

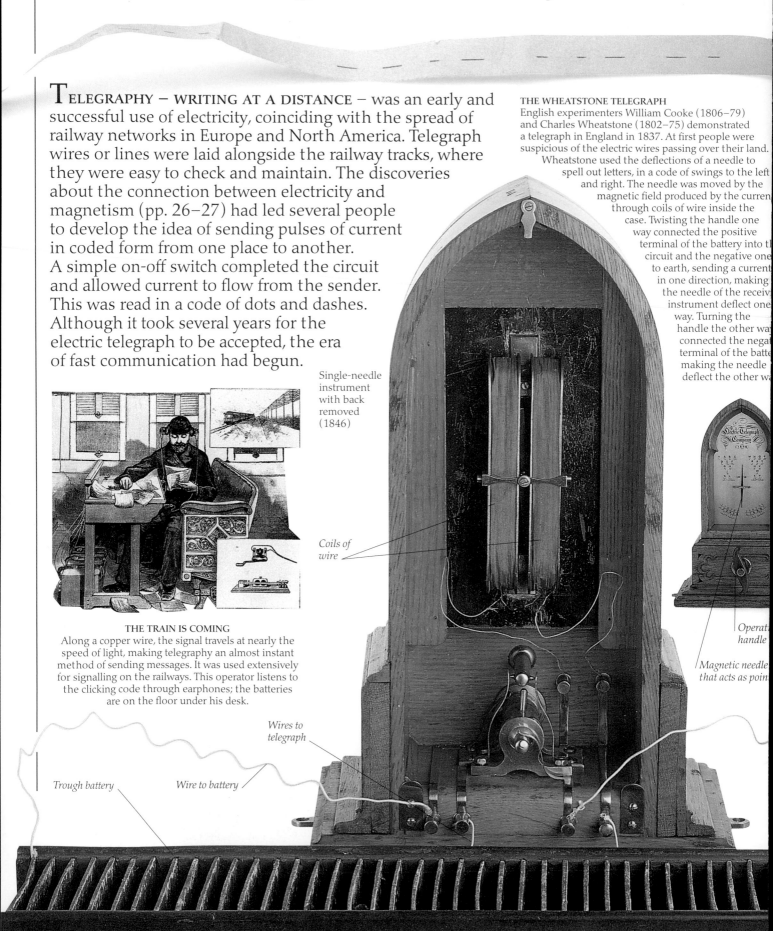

TELEGRAPHY – WRITING AT A DISTANCE – was an early and successful use of electricity, coinciding with the spread of railway networks in Europe and North America. Telegraph wires or lines were laid alongside the railway tracks, where they were easy to check and maintain. The discoveries about the connection between electricity and magnetism (pp. 26–27) had led several people to develop the idea of sending pulses of current in coded form from one place to another. A simple on-off switch completed the circuit and allowed current to flow from the sender. This was read in a code of dots and dashes. Although it took several years for the electric telegraph to be accepted, the era of fast communication had begun.

THE WHEATSTONE TELEGRAPH
English experimenters William Cooke (1806–79) and Charles Wheatstone (1802–75) demonstrated a telegraph in England in 1837. At first people were suspicious of the electric wires passing over their land. Wheatstone used the deflections of a needle to spell out letters, in a code of swings to the left and right. The needle was moved by the magnetic field produced by the current through coils of wire inside the case. Twisting the handle one way connected the positive terminal of the battery into the circuit and the negative one to earth, sending a current in one direction, making the needle of the receiving instrument deflect one way. Turning the handle the other way connected the negative terminal of the battery, making the needle deflect the other way.

Single-needle instrument with back removed (1846)

Coils of wire

THE TRAIN IS COMING
Along a copper wire, the signal travels at nearly the speed of light, making telegraphy an almost instant method of sending messages. It was used extensively for signalling on the railways. This operator listens to the clicking code through earphones; the batteries are on the floor under his desk.

Operating handle

Magnetic needle that acts as pointer

Wires to telegraph

Trough battery

Wire to battery

A .-	J .---	S ...	2 ..---
B -...	K -.-	T -	3 ...--
C -.-.	L .-..	U ..-	4 ....-
D -..	M --	V ...-	5 .....
E .	N -.	W .--	6 -....
F ..-.	O ---	X -..-	7 --...
G --.	P .--.	Y -.--	8 ---..
H	Q --.-	Z --..	9 ----.
I ..	R .-.	1 .----	0 -----

Modern Morse code alphabet

The "father of the telegraph"

American Samuel Morse (1791–1872) began his career as a professional portrait painter. The idea for a telegraph came to him in 1832 when he saw an electromagnet on a ship returning from a European tour. He gave up painting and began to investigate electromagnetism. By 1837 he had devised electromagnetic transmitters and receivers, and the first version of the code of dots and dashes that took his name and eventually became used worldwide. Morse's first permanent telegraph line, spanning 60 km (37 miles) between Baltimore and Washington, USA, opened on 24 May 1844 with Morse's message, "What hath God wrought!"

Samuel Morse

TS AND DASHES

...rse's early designs for a receiver ...d an electromagnet and a stylus ... pressed a groove into a moving paper ... Later, there was an inking device ...31) for writing dots and dashes. Trained ...graphers listened to the receiver's ...ks on a sounding device, decoded the ...sage from these, and wrote it down.

Morse tapes received on the *Great Eastern* when it was laying the 1865 Atlantic cable

Battery

Relay

Transformer

Electromagnets

...erer

Wire to battery

WIRELESS RECEIVER
The wireless telegraph was an advance on telegraphy, based on electromagnetic waves. This was made possible by the early experiments of Heinrich Hertz (pp. 60–61) and the practical efforts of Guglielmo Marconi (p. 61). This wireless receiver was the same as the telegraphy receivers in that it used Morse code, but instead of a connection to a land line, it had a radio receiver, which used a coherer. The coherer contains filings that increase in conductivity when they are subjected to radio waves. The link between the radio signal and the sounder circuit is made by the relay, which uses electromagnets (pp. 30–31). It passes the on-off pattern of the received current to a new, more powerful circuit.

LONG-DISTANCE BUSINESS
Telegraph lines spread across the land. Their real importance was appreciated by businesses where investments and information could be received quickly. These wealthy businessmen no doubt await the 19th-century version of the latest stock market figures.

Talking with electricity

SOUND WAVES DO NOT TRAVEL VERY FAR in air, or very fast. As the telegraph system became established for sending messages in coded form, several inventors pursued the idea of using the complex pattern of sound waves from the voice to produce a corresponding pattern of electrical signals. These could be sent along a wire much farther, and faster, than sound waves in the air. At the other end, the electrical signals would be converted back to sound, to recreate the original speech. A receiver and transmitter at each end allowed both callers to speak and listen. Bell, Edison, and others succeeded in making such devices, which became known as telephones. Telegraphs retained their role of sending relatively simple messages.

ALEXANDER GRAHAM BELL
Born in Scotland, Alexander Graham Bell (1847–1922) emigrated to North America in 1870, where he became an outstanding figure in the education of the deaf. He found that different voice tones could vary the electrical signals flowing in a wire, by the process of electro-magnetic induction. He also realized that a varying signal could vibrate a flat sheet or diaphragm, and produce sound waves. The principle of the telephone was born.

Terminals

INSIDE A BELL TELEPHONE
The "candlestick" design (1878) came about due to the mistaken belief that a longer permanent magnet would be stronger than a short one. The same design (below) could function as a mouthpiece (the sound detector or microphone) or earpiece (the sound producer). Sound waves vibrate an iron diaphragm varying the magnetic field of the bar magnet, which produces varying currents in the coil by electromagnetic induction. The principle of the earpiece design changed little from Bell's time until the 1970s, though improved materials allowed the permanent magnet inside the earpiece to be smaller. It is Edison's carbon microphone that is still used for the typical mouthpiece.

Bell's first telephone

THE FIRST CALL
With advice from Joseph Henry (p. 35), Bell and his assistant Thomas Watson constructed early versions of the telephone. Sound waves from the speaker's voice funnelled into a chamber, where they vibrated a flat sheet of thin iron, the diaphragm. This disturbed the magnetic field of a permanent magnet, around which was wrapped a current-carrying coil connected to an external battery. The magnetic field induced varying electrical signals in the circuit, which was completed through a connection to the earth.

The two-part telephone in use

Signal-carrying wire

Permanent bar magnet

Wooden casing

Coil of wire

Diaphragm

Funnel for sound waves

OPERATOR SERVICE
Only a few years after the first telephones were demonstrated, exchanges were being set up in major cities. The caller's plug had to be inserted into the correct socket. This is Croydon Exchange, near London, which opened in 1884.

...CEIVER PRINCIPLE
...an earpiece,
...anging signals
...w through the coils
...d set up a varying
...ctromagnetic field,
...ich interacts with
...e bar magnet's
...ady field. The
...erall fluctuating
...gnetic field attracts
...e iron diaphragm
... varying amounts,
...us vibrating it.

Signals from transmitter

Magnetic coil

Iron diaphragm

Sound waves

CARBON MICROPHONE
In a mouthpiece, a "button"
of loosely packed carbon
granules is connected into
a circuit with a battery.
Sound waves compress
and expand the carbon
granules, so decreasing
and increasing its
resistance, which varies
the electrical current.

Sound waves

Battery

Signals to receiver

Iron diaphragm

Carbon granules

Cutaway of 1920s
telephone handset

Permanent magnet

...ire coils

...aphragm

Gap

Signal-carrying wire

Carbon-granule button

Cotton wool pads

Diaphragm

Perforated screen

INSIDE AN EARPIECE
In this earpiece,
twin wire coils act as
electromagnets to vary
the magnetic field of the
permanent magnet.
The gap between the
diaphragm and magnet
is critical. It should allow the
diaphragm to vibrate sufficiently so the sound waves can
be heard, but not let the diaphragm touch the magnet.

INSIDE A MOUTHPIECE
In the mouthpiece
the perforated screen
protects the thin
diaphragm underneath
while still allowing
sound waves to pass
through. The carbon-
granule "button" is
surrounded by cotton wool
pads that allow the diaphragm
to vibrate freely while keeping
the grains of carbon in place.

Earpiece

...ank handle
...generator to
...duce current
...ing bell

Mouthpiece

Shaft

Magnet

...gnet

MAKING A CALL
This telephone
from 1895 contains a
small hand-operated
generator. When
callers wished to
alert the exchange,
they turned
the handle and
generated a small
electric current,
which produced
a signal for the
operator by ringing
a bell. A battery
situated nearby
provided current
for the microphone.
From about 1905
exchanges became
equipped with
batteries and ringing
equipment, so the
hand-generator
design faded out.

Connecting block
with terminals for
battery and line

Reed

Brass cylinder containing
carbon granules

Small pair
of coils

Electromagnet

THE BROWN REPEATER
From the 1900s electromechanical
repeaters were devised to copy the
pattern of telephone signals into another
circuit to make it stronger. In the Brown
repeater, the incoming signals flowed
through two small coils, producing
varying magnetic fields. These
vibrated a flexible metal
strip called a reed. The
reed was linked to a
small brass cylinder
containing carbon
granules, which
altered the current
in the new circuit.

Communicating without wires

James Clerk Maxwell (1831–79) developed the findings of Faraday and other scientists, using concepts such as magnetic lines of force, and reduced the phenomena of electricity and magnetism to a group of four mathematical equations. One prediction from these equations was that an oscillating electric charge would send out "waves" of electromagnetic energy from its source. A series of experiments by Heinrich Hertz (1857–94) in the 1880s demonstrated that these waves existed, and that they could be detected at a distance. Further work by Guglielmo Marconi (1874–1937) in the 1890s resulted in wireless telegraphy, the sending of messages without wires.

JAMES CLERK MAXWELL
Scottish-born Maxwell predicted the existence of radio waves before they were demonstrated by Hertz (below). He showed that an oscillating electric charge would produce a varying electromagnetic field, which would transmit at a speed that turned out to be equal to the speed of light. From this, he suggested that light rays were electro-magnetic waves.

HERTZ'S EXPERIMENTS
Hertz demonstrated the existence of radio waves in the late 1880s. He used a device called an induction coil to produce a high voltage. One of his early transmitters consisted of two tiny coils with a spark gap. The rapidly oscillating current in the sparks between the ends of the coils produced radio waves. To detect the waves Hertz used a receiver consisting of two rods with a spark gap as the receiving aerial. A spark jumped the gap where the waves were picked up. Hertz showed that these signals had all the properties of electromagnetic waves. They could be focused by curved reflectors, and a grid of parallel wires placed in their path showed they were polarized.

Heinrich Hertz

Transmitter

Receiver

Spark appeared between coils

Induction coil produced high voltage

Polarizing screen

Radio waves

Plane reflector

Replica of Hertz's equipment

Two coils and spark gap

Reflector

Polarizing screen

GUGLIELMO MARCONI

Marconi began radio experiments on his family's estate near Bologna, Italy. He devised arrangements of long wires and metal plates to emit and receive the waves. These were the first aerials. His first radio message across the Atlantic, from Cornwall in England to Newfoundland in Canada on December 1901, was Morse code for the letter S. It established the ability of radio for long-distance communication. Here, Marconi (left) shows some of his equipment to visitors in 1920.

ELECTRICITY INTO SOUND ENERGY

Headphones were used to listen to the first radio sets. Loudspeakers were then developed so that several people could listen at once. Loudspeakers needed radios with better detectors and amplifiers. This became possible when the triode valve was devised in 1906 by Lee De Forest (1873–1961) since the valve could amplify weak signals. The loudspeaker has a strong permanent magnet shaped like a cylinder. A coil of wire fits between the poles of the magnet within the strong magnetic field, and is attached to the cardboard cone. The varying electric currents pass through the coil making it move to and fro. As the coil moves, the cone moves, making sound waves that correspond to the varying electric currents.

Permanent magnet and coil in casing

Cone made from cardboard

How a loudspeaker works

Loudspeaker

Cylindrical magnet produces strong magnetic field

Varying currents passing through coil of wire vibrate cone, causing sound waves

RADIO RECEIVER

This state-of-the-art radio dates from 1925 and shows that large multi-wound aerials were required to gather the energy represented by radio waves. Each stage of circuitry in the receiver had to be individually tuned to the radio station.

The aerial frame can be rotated to produce the strongest signals

Aerial

Receiver in curved reflector

Rods pick up radio waves

Volume control

Tuning knob

Headphone socket

Touch-sensitive screen responds to tiny pulses of electricity

MODERN WIRELESS

Devices such as mobile phones, tablets, laptops, desk computers, media players such as iPods, and other gadgets use various forms of "wireless" or "wi-fi" technology – that is, radio waves. Mobile phones communicate with nearby masts to carry voice calls, Internet, and other information. Wireless printers, headphones, games controllers, and similar devices often use a much shorter-range radio system known as Bluetooth.

Television

IN THE AREA OF COMMUNICATION, there was another great aim for researchers and inventors. This was the wireless transmission not only of sounds, but of images too – television. Several systems were tried for turning patterns of light into electrical signals in the camera, transmitting and receiving the signals as radio waves, and displaying the received signals as a moving image for the viewer. A version of the vacuum tube, the cathode ray tube (CRT), became established as the image-displaying unit. This device was yet another stage in the two centuries of research, manipulation, and utilization of electricity – a form of energy that has become master and servant, indispensable and central to modern scientific thought.

INSIDE A 1930s TV SET
Many of the major electrical components described in this book, or their descendants, are contained in this electrical machine. The transformer and associated components produce high voltage which drive electrons in beams from the cathode through the anodes and towards the screen (pp. 54–55). The screen has a special coating so that it fluoresces white when the electrons hit it. Variable capacitors (p. 13) and other items tune the set to receive signals from different transmitters.

Deflection coil

Screen

Cathode ray tube

Control knobs

Loudspeaker

Capacitor

BAIRD'S MECHANICAL SCANNER
The television transmission equipment devised in the 1920s by John Logie Baird (1888–1946) was built using various bits of scrap metal and electrical components. Central was the Nipkow disc, a fast-spinning disc with holes arranged in a spiral. As the disc turned, each hole traced a curved line and exposed part of the scene behind. A photoelectric cell (p. 53) transformed the light intensity of each part of the line into electrical signals, and sent them to the receiver. Baird's 1926 version produced a 30-line image which was renewed 10 times each second. This electromechanical system was replaced by a purely electrical one (opposite).

the black-and-white television, electrons are produced at
cathode and are accelerated towards the positive electrode, the
de. They pass through holes in the anode, and are focused by
magnetic field produced by focusing coils to produce a spot
the screen. These pairs of focusing coils, one pair arranged
tically and the other horizontally, create fields that deflect the
ctron beam. The fields are varied so the beam sweeps across
screen, jumps back, sweeps an adjacent line, and so on to
er the screen. At the same time, the intensity of the beam is
ied by a signal applied to another electrode near the cathode.
en the beam is stronger, it makes the screen glow more brightly
he spot it hits. Each second, 25 complete pictures or frames are
duced. The human eye cannot follow the rapid movement of
electron beam and perceives a smoothly changing picture.

Electron beam

Four coils

Cathode

Anode

Vacuum tube

Scanned horizontal lines

cusing coil

Electron gun

*Insulated wire carries
very high voltage*

Resistor

Transformer

ZWORYKIN'S CONTRIBUTIONS
Many scientists contributed
to the cathode ray tube television
system. Vladimir Zworykin (1889–1982)
was born in Russia and moved to the USA
in 1919. In the 1920s he devised the iconoscope, which
used the scanning principle to convert visual images
into electrical signals, and he developed the use
of cathode ray tubes for displaying the images.
The first regular television broadcasts began
in 1936 in London, with each picture frame
composed of 405 horizontal lines. Later
525 lines were standard. Flat-screen
HDTVs (High Definition) have the
equivalent of more than 1,000 lines,
for a sharper, clearer picture.

The electronic age

An understanding of the behaviour and nature of electrons led to electronic
components such as the valve (p. 55). This was an enormous breakthrough
in communications but it relied on heat, wasting a great deal of energy, and
it was relatively fragile. During the late 1940s the first transistors were
developed. Transistors were used for
similar purposes as valves, and soon
replaced them for many applications. In
the 1960s techniques were introduced
to etch whole networks of components
on to a thin wafer or "chip" of silicon,
to make integrated circuits.

DIODE VALVE
The experimental Fleming diodes
of 1904 were the forerunners of
other types of vacuum tube, the
triode and pentode, with more
electrodes. Valves could use small
electrical signals and control the
current, and could thus amplify
radio signals (pp. 60–61).

TRANSISTOR
Like valves, transistors could
amplify electrical signals and
manipulate currents and
voltages in various ways.
But they were smaller, more
efficient, more robust, and
eventually cheaper than valves.

SILICON CHIP
A tiny wafer
of silicon
has circuits
containing
hundreds of
transistors and
other electrical
components.

Wafer of silicon

Did you know?

AMAZING FACTS

The electric eel is an unusual fish capable of generating powerful electrical shocks. Its shocks can keep predators away or stun an animal the eel is hunting for its own dinner. An adult can produce a shock of up to 500 volts; a juvenile gives a 100-volt strike.

Benjamin Franklin, credited with the invention of the lightning rod, worked for years to come up with the best design to "pull" lightning from the sky and direct it away from buildings. Some historians believe he began his famous kite-flying experiments because he was fed up with waiting for Christ Church in Philadelphia to be finished – he had planned to try out his lightning rod on the roof of the church.

Were batteries invented in Baghdad? In 1938, the director of the National Museum of Iraq wrote a paper speculating that an object dated to about 250 BCE was used to electroplate gold and silver coatings on certain objects. This object, known as the Baghdad Battery, resembles an electrochemical cell although there is no firm evidence to show how it was used.

"Lady Liberty" was a gift from France to the United States

Statue of Liberty

The International Space Station needs electricity to power its computers, light its interior, recycle water, and support life. But there is nowhere to plug it in! It gets its electricity from eight solar arrays, which extend from the station like huge wings. There are more than a quarter million solar cells in total on the arrays, used to capture solar power. When the ISS is orbiting in the Earth's shadow, it relies on rechargeable batteries.

Electricity travels almost at the speed of light – that's more than 299,000 km (186,000 miles) per second. If you could move that quickly, you could zip around the world nearly eight times in the same time it takes to flick on a light switch.

Introduced in 1946, the giant ENIAC (Electrical Numerical Integrator And Computer), one of the world's first computers, gobbled up 160 kilowatts of electrical power, weighed 30 tons, and covered 167 sq m (1,800 sq ft). On ENIAC's 50th anniversary, students at the University of Pennsylvania recreated the whole system on a microchip.

The first lighthouse in the United States to feature an electric light is also one of the most recognizable: the Statue of Liberty, in New York Harbour. The statue (officially decommissioned as a lighthouse in 1902) had a beam of light that was visible for 39 km (24 miles). Lady Liberty marks the entrance to the inner harbour of New York and the Hudson River.

When Thomas Edison's Pearl Street Station opened in New York in 1882, the station's lone generator produced enough electricity for 800 light bulbs. Today, the utility industry produces over 2.8 gigawatt-hours annually. That's enough to keep 50 billion low-energy bulbs (CFLs) lit up for an entire year.

The US White House was first wired for electricity in 1891. President Benjamin Harrison and his wife distrusted the switches so they used the original gas lamps, or asked staff to turn the electric ones on and off, or just left them on for days at a time.

ENIAC, with operator

The production of electricity from biomass (including animal wastes) is helping to meet increasing global energy needs. The waste produced by one chicken in a lifetime can supply enough energy to run a low-energy light bulb for 50 hours.

Ever wonder how birds can sit on power lines without getting an electric shock? Electricity always tries to make its way to the ground. If something is in the way (including you) it could travel through that thing to get there. But, normally, no part of a power line is "grounded" (touching the ground), so it is safe for birds to sit there.

Chicken

Birds on a wire

As late as 1993, high-tech electrical gadgets such as personal computers, printers, and video games had a negligible effect on the average American family's power usage. Today, however, these items are estimated to account for more than 13 per cent of a typical household energy budget, a figure that is expected to double by the year 2020.

QUESTIONS AND ANSWERS

Q What are the most common sources of electricity in the world today?

A Recent figures show coal is still the most common source, providing up to 40 per cent of electrical power. Natural gas contributes 20 per cent, hydropower 18 per cent, nuclear 11 per cent, oil 5 per cent, and renewables 6 per cent.

Q What are the nonrenewable sources used to make electricity?

A Coal and natural gas are considered fossil fuels, because they formed from the buried remains of plants and animals that lived millions of years ago. Uranium ore is not a fossil fuel, but it is mined and converted to a fuel used in nuclear power plants to make electricity. These energy sources are non-renewable because they cannot be replenished in a short period of time.

Q What are the renewable sources used to make electricity?

A Sources that can be replenished easily are called renewable energy sources. The five used most often around the world today are moving water, sunlight, wind, geothermal energy, and biomass.

Giant turbines at a wind farm, California, USA

Q What is hydropower? What are its advantages and disadvantages?

A Hydropower (energy derived from moving water) accounts for 7 per cent of US power generation and 45 per cent of renewable generation. It is considered by many the ideal fuel. It is free (apart from the cost of building the power plant), there are no waste products, and there is no pollution. But it can affect natural habitats, and can only be produced where there are ample amounts of moving water.

Q What is solar power, and what are its strengths and drawbacks?

A Sunlight can be converted directly or indirectly into other forms of energy. The term "solar power" usually refers to power created by solar panels, which use photovoltaic cells to convert sunlight directly into electricity. These panels have little impact on the environment and sunshine is free. The drawbacks are the large area needed to collect solar radiation at a useful rate, and the variable manner in which it arrives at the Earth's surface (clouds and fog can get in the way).

Solar energy can provide both warmth and electricity

Solar energy provides power for this building

Q How do we harness and use wind energy?

A Wind energy is harnessed using wind machines, highly advanced windmills made of high-strength materials. A typical wind machine stands as tall as a 20-storey building and has blades 60 m (200 ft) across. Wind is collected in a wind farm, a cluster of dozens of machines scattered over a large area. Wind farms need a lot of land, but animals can graze around the machines. The most serious drawbacks may be the impact on wild bird populations and the visual impact on the landscape.

Q What is geothermal energy?

A The Earth's interior contains geothermal (heat) energy. At a geothermal power plant, water is pumped down into the Earth's crust, where the heat causes it to evaporate – making steam that turns turbines to produce electricity. Other kinds of plant use steam that emerges naturally from the Earth in the form of geysers. It is only possible to build geothermal plants where there are unique geological conditions, but there is very little impact on the surrounding environment.

Q How is biomass used to make electricity?

A When you throw another log on the fire, you are making heat using biomass energy – energy released from burning organic material including wood, straw, animal wastes, garbage, and many other fuel sources. Utility companies are trying to develop ways to burn more biomass and less coal and natural gas to produce electricity. Some farmers grow burnable "energy crops" such as miscanthus grass.

Record Breakers

SOLAR POWER
Opened in 2012, the Gujarat PV Solar Park in India covers more than 3,000 acres (1,200 hectares) of desert and has a generating capacity of 600 MW (megawatts).

HYDROELECTRIC POWER
China's Three Gorges Dam across the Yangtze River is 2,335 m (7,660 ft) long and produces 22,000 MW of electricity.

WORLD'S SECOND LARGEST GEOTHERMAL PLANT
The Hellisheiði Power Station in Iceland is rated at 303 MW of electricity production.

Life without electricity

GOOD MORNING... OR IS IT?
If you are used to waking up with an electric alarm clock, you may oversleep. However, most clocks are fitted with back-up batteries to keep them ticking even if there is a power outage.

YOU HAVE JUST READ a basic history of electricity, giving you a better understanding of this force and the important role it plays in our world. But what if the imaginary "plug" to the world's electricity supply was suddenly pulled? We all know how inconvenient life seems when the power is cut for just a few hours. Our daily lives have become so dependent on electricity it is hard to believe that people ever lived without it. On these pages we will follow a typical day without power from the electric company. Of course, to live completely without electricity, we'd have to eliminate batteries and telephones as well – but we'll allow them for purposes of this section.

SWITCHED ON
The first thing most people reach for when they get out of bed is the light switch. But if the light doesn't come on when the switch is flicked, there are alternatives. Every household should have a supply of battery-operated flashlights. The most powerful models give out a great amount of bright light.

GETTING READY FOR THE DAY
Without a power source, the whirr of the electric toothbrush and the whine of the hairdryer won't be heard. We can't even run water into our homes without an electric pump, which helps us draw water – so showering, washing, doing laundry, or flushing the toilet would be impossible.

BREAKFAST TIME
You might start your day by blending up a smoothie or reaching into the fridge for something to toast or microwave. Without electricity, however, none of the appliances you have come to rely on will be on the menu. Food in your refrigerator will stay fresh for only a while if there is a power cut.

Candles provide a source of light, but must be used with care in the home

UP IN THE AIR
Air travel is severely disrupted without electricity. During major blackouts, airports may close or divert flights, causing chaos that takes days to fix.

RED LIGHT, GREEN LIGHT
Although schools would probably close during a prolonged power outage, you'd have a difficult time getting there in the first place. Traffic lights would not function, leading to gridlock due to traffic jams on the streets.

ALL ABOARD?
Many forms of public transport need electricity to keep people moving. City buses, subways, trolleys, and rail networks (such as Amtrak in the USA, shown above) would be forced to suspend or severely curtail their services without electricity, leaving many would-be travellers out of luck.

COOL IT, HEAT IT
Without electricity to power air conditioning or central heating units, you would have to either open a window or light a fire for temperature control. In earlier times, people chose their home sites based on issues of heating and cooling. They looked for valleys that gave shelter from the elements, and planted shady trees to keep the temperature down.

Dial-up Internet connections may work in power outages

HOME ENTERTAINMENT
Since going out during a power cut can be difficult, it may be best to stay at home. But how will you entertain yourself, without the Internet, computer games, cable television, or music? Battery-operated music players and hand-held computer games will keep you amused until the batteries run out. However, after that happens, you may play a card or board game, tell each other stories, or even read a book!

MORNING NEWS
Before electricity, information travelled at a much slower pace. People visited each other to exchange news. Today, most of us are used to flipping on the morning news on the radio, television, or surfing the Internet to get the top stories and local weather and travel updates. Unless you have a battery- or crank-operated gadget in the house, however, a power failure will leave you in the dark.

Switching a phone off conserves its power

POWER DOWN
A home emergency kit will be helpful in case of a temporary power outage. Flashlights (with extra batteries) and candles will provide a source of light, and a battery-operated radio will keep you in touch with the outside world. Stock up with store a first-aid kit as well as a non-electric can opener, some non-perishable food and snacks, and plenty of drinking water.

ON THE PHONE
During a power outage, cordless telephones will not work. Mobile phones, too, are only useful until their batteries run out – and that's assuming that their network is working. It's a good idea to keep a non-cordless phone in the house for emergencies.

Find out more

ELECTRICITY IS A FORCE THAT HAS TRANSFORMED the modern world. Here are some places to visit and things to do that will help you to understand why. Science museums contain plenty of exhibits to spark your knowledge about how electricity works. Many science centres feature fascinating hands-on exhibits that will enable you to experiment with electricity. Or, you could conduct simple experiments at home or at school. You might become the next Edison – if not, you can always visit his laboratory. Power plants, from your local station to a huge megaplant, may offer guided tours that will show you how electricity is made.

THOMAS EDISON'S LABORATORY
In the early 1900s, a team of 200 scientists and engineers filled the laboratory of American inventor Thomas Edison (above). His lab and home, now part of the National Park Service in New Jersey, USA, are now more likely to be bustling with tourists.

Cutaway of early electric kettle

VISIT A SCIENCE MUSEUM
For the past two centuries, scientists and inventors have had many bright ideas about electricity. Science museums contain many artefacts related to our understanding of electricity, as well as examples of early electrical appliances, such as this electric kettle from the 1920s.

Each hair repels the others. They stand on end to move as far away from each other as possible

MAKE A SCIENCE PROJECT
With just a few batteries, buzzers, and bulbs (and some wire and paper clips to connect them) you can explore the wonders of electricity. Your local library is an excellent source of step-by-step project books, from simple circuits to more complex machines and motors.

USEFUL WEBSITES

http://www.eia.gov/kids
The interactive kid's page of the US Energy Information Administration.

http://www.energykids.eu/
Fun activities help you explore and conserve energy.

http://www.nef.org.uk
The home of the National Energy Foundation

http://www.sparkmuseum.org/
Site of SPARK Museum of Electrical Invention, USA.

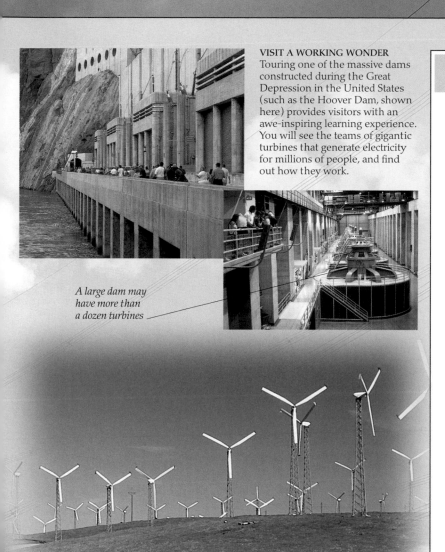

VISIT A WORKING WONDER
Touring one of the massive dams constructed during the Great Depression in the United States (such as the Hoover Dam, shown here) provides visitors with an awe-inspiring learning experience. You will see the teams of gigantic turbines that generate electricity for millions of people, and find out how they work.

A large dam may have more than a dozen turbines

Places to visit

SCIENCE MUSEUM, LONDON, UK
Visit to enjoy various hands-on exhibits and shows, including the Launchpad and "Energy: fuelling the future" gallery.

NATIONAL INVENTORS HALL OF FAME, VIRGINIA, USA
Learn more about American inventors and how they profoundly changed everyday life.

EXPLORATORIUM, SAN FRANCISCO, USA
A unique museum that lets children learn about science and art through experimentation.

BOSTON MUSEUM OF SCIENCE, BOSTON, USA
Get high-voltage thrills at this museum's live Theater of Electricity show.

DISCOVERY PLACE KIDS MUSEUMS, NORTH CAROLINA, USA
Several new Discovery Place KIDS locations across the region, appealing to families with young children.

GLASGOW SCIENCE CENTRE, GLASGOW, UK
There are more than 250 interactive science exhibits that you can have fun with, and plenty of games and experiments in the energy and forces category.

DEUTSCHES MUSEUM, MUNICH, GERMANY
Visit one of the world's largest museums of science and technology, and go to its Energy section to see electricity-related exhibits.

THE FRANKLIN INSTITUTE, PHILADELPHIA, USA
Watch a bolt of lightning strike and have a hair-raising experience at this superb science centre.

ST LOUIS SCIENCE CENTER, ST LOUIS, USA
This centre features more than 700 hands-on exhibits for you to explore and enjoy.

EUREKA! THE NATIONAL CHILDREN'S MUSEUM, HALIFAX, UK
Enjoy the many interactive exhibits and also special events that are organized through the year.

VISIT A WIND FARM
In some parts of the United States, you can ride through a "forest" of towering silver windmills on a wind farm tour. Guides will show you the gigantic machines used to harness the power of the wind, and explain how this ancient method of capturing energy could help limit our dependence on fossil fuels in the future. Check the Internet or a travel guide for details.

VISIT A SCIENCE CENTRE
Spending a day at an interactive science centre will get you charged up about electricity. These centres help you learn more about the concepts in this book through fascinating hands-on experimentation. Here, two boys get an electrical charge when they touch a Van de Graaff generator.

Touching the generator gives you a positive charge

TOUR A POWER PLANT
Take a behind-the-scenes tour of your local power plant, and you will find out how the electricity you use is produced. Many non-nuclear power plants conduct tours for school and community groups. Check the Internet for details. Due to security concerns, most power stations will require advance reservations for tours.

Glossary

AMBER A hard fossil of tree gum or resin that is yellowish to brownish in colour. The Greek word for amber, *elektron*, is the root of our word "electricity."

BATTERY A device that transforms chemical energy into electric energy. Originally, the term is applied to a group of two or more electric cells connected together. In common usage, the term "battery" now also applies to a single cell, such as the familiar household battery.

CAPACITOR A device which stores electrical energy, using a positively charged surface and a negatively charged surface with a gap between them. The Leyden jar was an early form of capacitor. Capacitors were formerly called condensers.

CATHODE RAY TUBE Cathode rays are streams of high-speed electrons emitted from the heated cathode of a vacuum tube. In a cathode ray tube, the electrons are carefully directed into a beam. This beam is deflected by a magnetic field to scan the surface of a screen, which is lined with phosphorescent material. When the electrons hit this material, light is emitted. Cathode ray tubes were used in most televisions, computer displays, and video monitors.

Cathode ray tube

CELL An electricity-making unit, which delivers an electrical current as the result of a chemical reaction – a household battery, for example.

CIRCUIT An electrical device that provides a path along which an electrical current can flow.

CONDENSER An old name for an electrical capacitor, now rarely used except in historical contexts.

CONDUCTOR Any material that allows electricity to move through it easily. Metals are especially good conductors.

CURRENT A measure of the flow of electrons moving past a certain point in a given time, usually through a metal wire or other conductor.

DIODE VALVE An electronic device with two electrodes or terminals, which conducts current flow in only one direction. In the late 1950s, diode valves began to be replaced by transistors.

DYNAMO Another name for an electrical generator.

ELECTRIC CHARGE A measure of the excess or deficiency of electrons in a given object or material.

ELECTRICITY A form of energy produced by the flow of negatively and positively charged particles of matter.

ELECTROCARDIOGRAPH A medical instrument that records electric currents associated with contractions of the heart.

ELECTROLYSIS The process of breaking a chemical compound down into its elements by passing a direct current through it. Electrolysis of water, for example, produces hydrogen and oxygen.

ELECTROMAGNET A coil of wire, usually wound on an iron core, which produces a strong magnetic field when an electric current is sent through it.

ELECTRON A negatively charged particle; one of the three basic kinds of particles that make up an atom.

ELECTROPHORUS A simple electrostatic generator that generates repeated charges of static electricity.

ELECTROPLATING The process of coating an electroconductive material with a thin layer of metal by passing an electric current through the material.

ELECTROSCOPE A device used to measure the electric charge of an object or material.

ELECTROSTATIC ATTRACTION The attractive force between two oppositely charged ions.

FILAMENT LAMP A type of incandescent lamp in which the light source is a fine electrical conductor heated by the passage of current.

FLUORESCENCE The emission of visible light by a substance, such as certain minerals, that is currently being exposed to ultraviolet light and absorbing radiation from it. The light appears in the form of glowing, distinctive colours.

GALVANOMETER An instrument used to measure small electric currents.

GENERATOR A machine that converts mechanical energy into electrical energy.

GEOTHERMAL ENERGY Energy derived from the internal heat of the Earth, which can be used to generate electricity.

HEATING ELEMENT The part of a heater or stove that transforms fuel or electricity into heat.

The display shows heart rate and blood pressure

Electrocardiograph machine

HYDROELECTRIC Refers to the process of using flowing water to create electricity.

INDUCTION The process of producing a magnetic charge through changes in an electric current flow.

INDUCTION COIL A coil for producing high voltage from a low-voltage source. It consists of a primary coil through which the direct current flows, an interrupter, and a secondary coil with more turns in which the high voltage is induced.

Cups act as terminals

Fabric insulation

Induction coil

INDUCTION MOTOR The simplest type of electric motor; converts electrical energy into mechanical energy using a rotating magnetic field.

Leyden jar

INSULATOR A material which resists the flow of electric current.

LEYDEN JAR A glass jar or bottle used to accumulate electricity. Coated with foil both inside and out, it is connected to a metal conducting rod, which passes through an insulating stopper and charges the jar with electricity.

MAGNETISM A property, possessed by certain materials, that attracts or repels similar materials. Magnetism is closely associated with moving electricity.

METER A device used to measure electricity use in a business or home.

MORSE CODE A communications system of letters coded into dots and dashes, sent as short electrical signals (dots) and long signals (dashes) along a telegraph line.

MOTOR A machine that converts electrical energy into mechanical energy.

PACEMAKER An electronic device which is surgically implanted into the heart and chest in order to control the heart's rhythm when it beats erratically.

PHOTOVOLTAIC CELL An electronic device that converts light to electricity.

POWER STATION An electrical generating station which sends energy directly into homes, offices, and factories.

PYLON A large steel tower which supports high-tension power lines.

RADIO The wireless transmission and reception of electric impulses or signals by means of electromagnetic waves.

RESISTANCE A material's opposition to the flow of electric current.

SCANNER An electrical device that images or records an object using a moving beam, line by line.

SELENIUM A light-sensitive element that occurs naturally in food and soils, and that generates electric current when exposed to light.

SILICON CHIP A wafer-thin slice of silicon that contains thousands of microscopic electronic circuits.

SOLAR POWER Sunlight that has been converted into thermal or electrical energy.

SPARK A short electrical discharge between two conductors.

STATIC ELECTRICITY An electrical charge that builds up due to friction between two dissimilar materials. Friction removes some electrons from one object and deposits them on the other.

STEP-DOWN TRANSFORMER A transformer that reduces voltage.

TELEGRAPH A mechanical or electrical apparatus used to communicate at a distance over a wire, usually through Morse code.

TELEPHONE An instrument used for voice communication that works by converting sound waves into electrical energy, and electrical energy into sound waves.

TELEVISION A form of communication that operates through the transmission of pictures and sounds in the form of electrical waves.

THERMOCOUPLE A device that produces a small voltage, which indicates a temperature difference between two metals.

TIDAL POWER Power obtained by the generation of electricity using changing ocean tides.

TRANSFORMER A device that changes electricity from one voltage to another.

TRANSISTOR A tiny electrical device used to amplify an electrical signal, which can be switched on and off to either aid or inhibit the flow of electrical current.

Water drives a massive turbine

Telegraph

TURBINE A device for converting the flow of a fluid (air, steam, water, or hot gases) into mechanical motion that in turn can be used to produce electricity.

VERSORIUM The earliest form of scientific electroscope, created by William Gilbert in 1600. Used to indicate the direction of an electronic force, the device consisted simply of a light metallic needle balanced on a pivot, similar to a compass.

VOLT A unit of electrical pressure which measures the force or push of electricity.

VOLTAIC PILE A device which uses different metals, separated by moist chemicals, to produce a flow of electric charge; a form of battery.

WATT A unit of electrical power used to indicate the rate of energy produced or consumed by an electrical device. One watt is equal to one joule of energy per second. The watt is named for James Watt, inventor of the modern steam engine.

XEROGRAPHY MACHINE Another name for the electrostatic printer, invented by Chester Carlson in 1938.

Index

Acknowledgements

The publisher would like to thank:
Fred Archer, Brian Bowers, Roger Bridgman, Janet Carding, Eryl Davies, Robert Excell, Graeme Fyffe, Derek Hudson, Dr Ghislaine Lawrence, Barry Marshall and the staff of the Museum Workshop; Douglas Millard, Victoria Smith, Peter Stephens, Peter Tomlinson, Kenneth Waterman, Anthony Wilson, and David Woodcock for advice and help with the provision of objects for photography at the Science Museum; Dave Mancini at Nortech and Peter Griffiths for the model making; Deborah Rhodes for page makeup, Peter Cooling for computer artwork; Robert Hulse for standing in for Michael Faraday and Humphry Davy; Karl Adamson and Tim Ridley for assistance with the photography; Jack Challoner for help in the initial stages of the book; Monica Byles for proofreading; and Helen Peters for indexing.

Picture research Deborah Pownall and Catherine O'Rourke
Illustrations Kuo Kang Chen

Picture credits
(Key: a-above; b-below/bottom; c-centre; f-far; l-left; r-right; t-top)
Ashmolean Museum, Oxford 8tr.
Bildarchiv Preussischer Kulturbesitz 40br.
Bridgeman Art Library 8bc; /Philips 32tl.
Bt Museum, London 8c; 58bl.
Hulton Picture Co. /Bettmann Archive 14tc; 16bc; 28tl; /Bettmann Archive 52tr; 56cl; 57br; 58cl; 58tl; 61tl; 62cl; /Bettmann Archive 63cr.
Getty Images: H. Armstrong Roberts/ Retrofile 58ccb, Encyclopaedia Britannica/ Universal Images Group 51br, What Laptop Magazine/Future 67br, Science & Society Picture Library 21bl, 36clb, Fstop/The Image Bank 70cr, Kenzo Triboullard/AFP 45cra Patsy Kelly 12–13.
Kobal Collection 12bl; 50cl.
Mansell Collection 6cl; 24cl; 47cr.
Mary Evans Picture Library 7cl; 15bl; 19c; 19c; 27tc; 30tr; 37cl; 41tr; 43tr; 44bl; 46tl; 46bl; 49cr; 61tr.
MIT Museum, Cambridge,

Massachusetts 12c.
National Portrait Gallery, London 10tr.
National Portrait Gallery, Washington 29tr.
NEI Parsons 42cr; 43bl.
Ann Ronan Picture Library 11tc; 19cb; 42tl; 51tr; 53tl.
Rover Group 33br.
Royal Institution, London 35tr; 35cr.
Science Museum Photo Library cover front tl; back tl; 9tr; 18tl; 23tl; 27clb; 29br; 34tl; 41tc; 48tr; 55cr; 57tr; 60clb.
Science Photo Library /Gordon Garrado cover front c; 7tr; /Simon Fraser 7cr; /David Parker 12bc; 29bl; /David Parker 31br; / Jean-Loup Charmet 43tc; Hank Morgan 45tr; /Gary Ladd 45crb; 52bl; 53br; / Jean-Loup Charmet 54bl. Wellcome Institute Library 24crb.
Zefa 41br.
Alamy: Photofusion Picture Library 71tr.
Corbis: Anamitra Chakladar / Demotix 31br; Paul Souders / Jochen Tack / imagebroker 7cr; Paul Almasy 65br; Lester V. Bergman 68br; Bettman Collection 64tr, 68tl.

PITCHAL FREDERIC 69bcr; Charles Gupton 69c; Eric and David Hosking 64br; Gunter Marx Photography 68tl; Sally A. Morgan, Ecoscene 65tr; Joseph Sohm ctl Getty Images: AFP 68br; National Geographic 69cr Chrissy McIntyre: 68cl Science Photo Library/Photo Researchers: 68bl

With the exception of the items listed above and the objects on pages 6, 22, 25, 31c, 33t, 49c, 52, 53t, all the photographs in this book are of objects in the collections of the Science Museum, London.

Wallchart: Corbis: Radius Images bl; Dorling Kindersley: ESA tr, The Science Museum, London c, cl, cra, cr, cb, cb/ (thermocouple), clb, bc; Getty Images: Encyclopaedia Britannica / Universal Images Group crb, DaveArnoldPhoto.com / Flickr tl

All other images © Dorling Kindersley
For further information see:
www.dkimages.com